THE WOKE PARENT:
THE NEW AGE MUNCHAUSEN BY PROXY

Frimpong Conveycase

© Copyright 2024 by

Publishing

Dedicated to:

My son, Riley Conveycase.

Table of Contents

Introduction

1. Leane's Story and the Modern Phenomenon of Parenting as Performance
2. Social Media's Influence on Parenting Decisions
3. Parental Motivations and Munchausen by Proxy in the Digital Era
4. The Consequences of Exploiting Children's Identities

Chapter 1: The Digital Stage: Where Parenting Becomes Performance

I. Introduction: Parenting in the Age of Public Performance
II. Leanne's Story: A Parent's Journey on the Digital Stage

- A. From Private Concern to Public Spectacle
- B. The Online Reaction: Support and Criticism
  III. When Support Becomes Exploitation
  IV. The New Face of Munchausen by Proxy
  V. A Cautionary Tale: When Children Become Symbols
  VI. The Role of Social Media in Medicalization
  VII. Setting the Stage for the Journey Ahead
  VIII. Conclusion: A Call for Change

Chapter 2: The Shifting Landscape of Gender Identity and Cultural Change

I. Introduction: A Decade of Transformation
II. The Rise of Non-Binary and Fluid Gender Identities

- A. Expanding the Language of Gender
- B. Social Media's Role in Amplifying New Identities
- C. The Decoupling of Gender Identity from Medical Transition
  III. 2015: A Year of Cultural Overhaul
  IV. Language as a Tool of Ideological Change
  V. Identity-Based Hiring and Education: The Rise of Affirmative Action 2.0
  VI. The Evolution of LGBTQ+ Rights and the Expansion of Pride
  VII. A Shifting Landscape: The Impact on Language, Culture, and Society
  VIII. Conclusion: A New Understanding of Identity in the 21st Century

---

Chapter 3: How Social Media Amplified Woke Ideology

I. Introduction: The Digital Megaphone—From Margins to Mainstream
II. Algorithms and the Weaponization of Outrage
III. From Awareness to Orthodoxy: The Role of Influencers and Activists
IV. Creating Echo Chambers: How Social Media Shapes Perception
V. Turning Children into Political Symbols
VI. The Role of Social Media in Medicalization
VII. Conclusion: A Call for Digital Responsibility

Chapter 4: Narcissism in the Digital Age

I. Introduction: Understanding Narcissism in Modern Parenting
II. Defining Narcissism and Its Manifestations
III. The Role of Validation in Reinforcing Behavior
IV. Linking Narcissism and Munchausen by Proxy
V. The Role of Validation in Parenting Dynamics
VI. Manipulation and Control: When Parenting Crosses the Line
VII. Ideological Munchausen by Proxy: A New Form of Child Exploitation
VIII. The Long-Term Consequences of Parental Narcissism
IX. Conclusion: Safeguarding Children's Emotional and Psychological Health

---

Chapter 5: The Story of Leane and the Disturbing Trend of Ideological Parenting

I. Introduction: Leane's Controversial Story
II. Phases vs. Permanent Changes: A Child's Natural Exploration
III. The Role of Social Media and Ideological Echo Chambers
IV. From Phases to Permanent Consequences: Ignoring the Child's Natural Growth
V. Pharmaceutical Influence and the Corporate Agenda
VI. A Metaphor for Today: The Boy Who Identified as a Vulture
VII. Ideological Parenting: A Risky Path for the Child
VIII. Conclusion: The Need for Caution and Responsibility

Chapter 6: Stories of Regret: Children Who Detransitioned and Feel Manipulated by Their Parents

I. Introduction: The Hidden Voices of Detransitioners
II. The Case of Chloe Cole: A Voice for Detransitioners
III. Regret and Reversal: Helena Kerschner's Story
IV. The Role of Social Media and Peer Influence in Shaping Identity
V. Expert Concerns and Calls for Caution

VI. A Call for Thoughtful Individualized Care
VII. Conclusion: Listening to the Voices of Regret

Chapter 7: The State's Role in Gender Ideology

I. Introduction: A New Frontier of Parental Control
II. Policies of Secrecy: Undermining Parental Authority
III. Criminalizing Parental Objections: Legal Consequences and Loss of Custody
IV. Redefining Family: The State's Growing Influence on Parenting
V. Media and Institutional Influence: Shaping Public Perception
VI. Incremental Erosion of Parental Rights: A Slippery Slope
VII. A Call for Balance: Reaffirming the Role of the Family
VIII. Conclusion: Reclaiming the Family's Role in Child Development

Chapter 8: Legal Battles and Custody Wars

I. Introduction: The Gender Divide in Custody Battles
II. Weaponizing the System: Ideology in Custody Disputes
III. The Case of Ted Hudacko: A Father's Struggle for Rights
IV. A System Rigged Against Fathers: The Broader Trend
V. Real-Life Cases: Fathers on the Losing Side
VI. A Call for Reform: Ensuring Fairness in Custody Battles
VII. Conclusion: Reaffirming the Role of Both Parents

Chapter 9: The Intersection of Medicine, Government, and Profit

I. Introduction: When Health Becomes a Commodity
II. The Pharmaceutical Industry's Role in Gender Transitioning
III. Government Involvement: Policies That Promote Profit Over Caution
IV. The Profit Motive in Medicine: From Treatment to Commodity
V. The Ethical Dilemma: Medicine or Market?
VI. Government Contracts and the Influence of Big Pharma
VII. A Call for Reform: Protecting Patients Over Profit
VIII. Conclusion: Prioritizing Health Over Profit

Chapter 10: The Emotional and Psychological Toll

I. Introduction: Childhood Transitions—A Complex Terrain
II. Understanding Childhood and Adolescent Psychology
III. The Emotional Toll of Early Transitions
IV. Stories of Regret: Voices of Detransitioners
V. Social Isolation and the Reality of Transitioning
VI. The Impact of Emotional Manipulation and Ideological Pressure
VII. A Call for Responsibility: Protecting Vulnerable Children
VIII. Conclusion: A Call for Caution and Compassion

Chapter 11: Stories of Detransitioners

I. Introduction: The Hidden Voices of Detransitioners
II. Understanding Detransition: What It Means and Why It Matters
III. The Physical and Physiological Challenges of Detransitioning
IV. Emotional and Psychological Challenges
V. Case Studies of Detransitioners: Real Stories, Real Consequences
VI. The Lack of Support and Resources for Detransitioners
VII. Moving Forward: A Call for a More Cautious Approach
VIII. Conclusion: Listening to the Voices of Detransitioners

Chapter 12: Restoring Balance: Parental Rights, Responsibility, and Children's Well-Being

I. Introduction: The Foundation of Family
II. Strengthening Parental Rights: The Need for Transparency and Oversight
III. The Importance of Active Involvement: Being Present and Aware
IV. The Role of Schools: Restoring the Purpose of Education
V. The Economic Impact: How Financial Pressures Affect Family Dynamics
VI. The Fight for Autonomy in Child-Rearing
VII. Prioritizing Children's Well-Being: A Balanced Approach
VIII. Conclusion: Reaffirming Parental Guidance and Family Values

Chapter 13: Guiding Children in Understanding Gender Identity, Responsibility, and Societal Roles

I. Introduction: Navigating Complexities of Identity
II. A Balanced Approach to Teaching Gender Differences
III. Keeping Political Ideology Out of Education
IV. Liberty, Responsibility, and Understanding Societal Roles
V. Reintroducing Practical Skills and Civic Education

VI. Restoring Parental Involvement and Building Strong Families
VII. Conclusion: A Path Toward Balance and Stability

Chapter 14: Addressing the Issue of Medical Protocols and Protecting Children from Ideological Manipulation

I. Introduction: Establishing Safe Medical Practices
II. Common-Sense Medical Guidelines for Children
III. The Influence of Ideology on Medical Decisions
IV. The Dangers of Social and Ideological Engineering
V. The Intersection of Ideology and Infrastructure
VI. Protecting Children from Ideological Manipulation
VII. Standing Firm Against Ideological Intimidation
VIII. Conclusion: Ensuring a Safe Future for Our Children

Introduction

In a digital world where every moment can be captured, shared, and scrutinized, parenting has entered uncharted territory. No longer confined to private decisions made within the home, the choices parents make about their children's upbringing are now subject to public judgment, applause, and condemnation. Social media has transformed parenting into a spectator sport, where the stakes are measured not just in terms of a child's well-being, but in terms of likes, followers, and validation.

One such example of this phenomenon recently surfaced on TikTok, igniting a firestorm of controversy and debate. A mother, whom we'll call **Leanne**, posted a series of videos declaring that her two-year-old was transgender. She narrated, with an air of earnest confidence, that her toddler was able to communicate the truth about his/ her identity to her. Leanne believed that she was doing what any good parent should—listening to her child and supporting them as they navigated their path to self-discovery.

Leanne's story quickly went viral. It was viewed millions of times, with thousands of comments pouring in, divided between praise and outrage. Supporters called her a trailblazer, applauding her courage and progressive values. Detractors, however, were aghast. How could a child so young, they argued, possibly grasp the complexities of gender identity? Was this truly about the child's welfare, or was it about the mother's need for attention? These questions led to an even darker possibility: Could this be a modern manifestation of **Munchausen by proxy**, a disorder in which caregivers fabricate or exaggerate medical conditions in those under their care to gain sympathy and attention?

Chapter 1: The Digital Stage: Where Parenting Becomes Performance

Objectives for the Reader:

1. **Understand the Shift in Parenting Dynamics Due to Social Media:**
   - Explore how social media platforms like TikTok, Instagram, and YouTube have transformed private parenting into a public performance, where parental decisions are now subject to public scrutiny and validation.
2. **Analyze a Case Study of Parental Performance:**
   - Gain insight into Leanne's story as a case study that illustrates the transformation from private parenting concerns to a highly publicized performance influenced by online feedback and validation.
3. **Examine the Ethical Implications of Public Parenting:**
   - Reflect on the ethical concerns of sharing a child's personal journey online and how this shift has changed the role of parents from guides to public narrators of their children's lives.
4. **Identify the Risks of Early Medical Interventions for Public Validation:**
   - Discuss the pressure on parents to pursue early medical interventions for their children, driven by online praise, social approval, and the desire to appear progressive.
5. **Explore the Concept of Digital Munchausen by Proxy:**
   - Introduce the idea of "Digital Munchausen by Proxy" in which parents manipulate a child's identity for online attention and sympathy, raising concerns about potential harm and exploitation.
6. **Evaluate the Consequences for Children in the Public Eye:**
   - Understand the long-term effects on children whose identities become public symbols in cultural debates, leading to possible identity confusion and psychological distress.
7. **Analyze the Role of Social Media in the Medicalization of Childhood:**
   - Investigate how social media pressure can influence parental decisions to pursue medical interventions and how the intersection of ideology and industry can complicate the ethics of such choices.
8. **Highlight the Need for Digital Responsibility:**
   - Encourage a balanced and responsible use of social media by parents, with a focus on protecting children's privacy and prioritizing their well-being over public validation.
9. **Call for Change in the Digital Era of Parenting:**
   - Advocate for a shift in how society views digital parenting, urging influencers, parents, and the broader community to put the child's well-being first and avoid turning them into symbols of broader cultural battles.

Chapter 1: The Digital Stage: Where Parenting Becomes Performance

I. Introduction: Parenting in the Age of Public Performance

In the past, parenting was a private endeavor, with decisions made discreetly in the company of close family members and trusted professionals. Parents faced difficult choices in solitude, often struggling to navigate complex issues behind closed doors. Today, however, social media has shattered that privacy, transforming parenting into a public spectacle.

Platforms like TikTok, Instagram, and YouTube serve as digital stages, where parents broadcast their children's lives to a global audience. From mundane daily routines to deeply personal choices about identity and health, everything is shared, documented, and evaluated by an unseen online audience. As a result, parenting has become a form of performance, where every action, decision, and update can be judged, validated, or criticized.

II. Leanne's Story: A Parent's Journey on the Digital Stage

Leanne's story is a prime example of how quickly a personal narrative can escalate into a public spectacle. What began as a well-intentioned effort to support her child soon turned into a performance, influenced by the constant feedback of likes, shares, and comments from strangers online.

- **A. From Private Concern to Public Spectacle** At first, Leanne shared small glimpses of her child's gender exploration, posting updates about consultations with doctors and gender specialists. Encouraged by positive reactions and growing online support, she started documenting more of her child's journey, eventually sharing every milestone and decision about future medical interventions.
- **B. The Online Reaction: Support and Criticism** As Leanne's videos gained traction, the feedback became polarized. Supporters praised her as a loving, affirming parent, while critics accused her of exploiting her child for social media clout. This dichotomy blurred the true nature of her actions. Was she genuinely advocating for her child, or was she subconsciously using the platform to gain validation for herself?

III. When Support Becomes Exploitation

Leanne's case is part of a larger trend that raises critical questions about the ethics of publicly sharing a child's personal journey. The nature of parental roles has shifted—parents are no longer just guides but directors of public narratives.

- **A. The Transformation of Parental Roles** In these scenarios, parents showcase their child's "bravery" and their own "courage" as supportive figures. What should be a private family matter often turns into a public statement, with children becoming symbols in ideological battles rather than individuals on a personal journey.

- **B. Early Medical Interventions: Rushing Decisions for Public Validation** Many parents, influenced by online praise and the desire to appear progressive, opt for early medical interventions such as puberty blockers or hormone therapy. However, these decisions—often irreversible—are made in the spotlight, without allowing children the time and space to explore their identities away from public scrutiny.

IV. The New Face of Munchausen by Proxy

The digital age has given rise to a modern form of Munchausen by proxy, where a parent uses a child's identity rather than a physical illness to gain attention and sympathy.

- **A. Redefining Munchausen by Proxy in the Digital Era** Traditionally, Munchausen by proxy involved fabricating or inducing medical symptoms in a child. In the context of social media, the "condition" becomes the child's gender identity. The more dramatic the narrative—the younger the child, the bolder the intervention—the greater the response from online communities.
- **B. A Condition Celebrated Rather Than Hidden** Unlike traditional cases that remain hidden until uncovered by medical professionals, this new form is displayed and celebrated publicly, making it difficult to discern genuine support from potentially harmful behavior. The digital stage allows for harmful patterns to go unchecked, as parents are praised rather than scrutinized.

V. A Cautionary Tale: When Children Become Symbols

Leanne's story—and others like it—serves as a cautionary tale. It shows the danger of turning children into symbols of broader cultural battles. These narratives place immense pressure on young individuals, often before they can fully grasp the implications of being in the public eye.

- **A. Real-Life Consequences for Children** Children thrust into the spotlight often grow up feeling trapped in identities shaped more by their parents and online communities than by their own experiences. As they mature, some may regret decisions made during early childhood, leading to feelings of betrayal.
- **B. The Pressure to Uphold a Public Role** Once a child's identity becomes a public story, it's nearly impossible to step back. Parents, fearful of losing their newfound status and support, may continue pushing the narrative, trapping the child in a role they may no longer want to play.

VI. The Role of Social Media in Medicalization

Social media's influence extends beyond shaping beliefs—it shapes actions. Parents who gain online attention for their child's gender exploration often feel pressured to escalate to medical interventions.

- **A. Online Pressure to Move Beyond Social Support** The narrative of "bravery" online can push parents to pursue hormone therapy or puberty blockers, believing it's the next

step to show their unconditional support. Social media often presents these decisions as the only compassionate option, ignoring potential risks and long-term consequences.
- **B. The Intersection of Ideology and Industry** Clinics and pharmaceutical companies see increased demand as these narratives become more visible. The intersection of ideology and industry creates a troubling dynamic where validation and profit can override caution and thorough evaluation.

VII. Setting the Stage for the Journey Ahead

This chapter sets the groundwork for deeper exploration into the impact of woke ideology, social media, and parental motivations.

- **A. Understanding the Motivations of Parents** Analyzing why some parents are drawn to publicly display their children's journeys.
- **B. Examining the Impact on Children** Assessing the short- and long-term effects on children caught in the spotlight.
- **C. A Call for Digital Responsibility** Encouraging a balanced perspective that respects children's privacy and prioritizes their well-being.

VIII. Conclusion: A Call for Change

- **A. Protecting Children from Becoming Symbols** Social media has the power to elevate or exploit—parents, influencers, and society must recognize the difference.
- **B. Putting the Child First** As we navigate the complexities of identity in a digital age, the child's well-being must remain at the forefront of every decision.

Chapter 2: The Shifting Landscape of Gender Identity and Cultural Change - Reader Objectives

1. **Understand the Evolution of Gender Identity:**
   - Gain insight into how the understanding and language of gender identity have transformed from traditional male and female roles to a spectrum of fluid identities.
   - Explore the rise of non-binary and gender-fluid identities and how these concepts have shaped modern discussions around identity.
2. **Examine the Influence of Social Media:**
   - Learn about the critical role of social media platforms in amplifying and accelerating changes in gender identity discourse.
   - Analyze how platforms like Tumblr, Twitter, and others have created spaces for marginalized communities to explore and share their experiences.
3. **Explore the Impact of Cultural and Linguistic Changes:**
   - Review the emergence of cancel culture, changes in language, and the rebranding of cultural symbols to reflect new societal norms.
   - Assess how language has been used as a tool for ideological change and the implications this has for society.
4. **Evaluate Identity-Based Hiring and Education Practices:**
   - Understand the shift from merit-based evaluations to identity-based hiring and admissions.
   - Consider the consequences—both intended and unintended—of prioritizing identity over traditional measures of merit.
5. **Trace the Evolution of LGBTQ+ Rights and Representation:**
   - Learn how the LGBTQ+ movement has expanded from a focus on gay and lesbian rights to a broader spectrum of identities.
   - Analyze the controversial expansion of Pride celebrations and the tensions around public representation and appropriateness.
6. **Assess the Broader Societal Shifts:**
   - Explore the broader cultural shifts in language, hiring practices, and societal expectations brought about by these evolving norms.
   - Consider the polarization and backlash that have resulted from rapid changes and the cultural divide it has created.
7. **Navigate the Complexity of Inclusivity and Societal Balance:**
   - Reflect on the complexities of balancing inclusivity with societal cohesion.
   - Explore questions around creating an inclusive society without alienating those who struggle to adapt to these new norms.
8. **Prepare for Future Discussions on Identity and Social Change:**
   - Gain a foundation for understanding the evolving nature of identity and social change in the 21st century.
   - Recognize the importance of maintaining a balanced perspective that respects diverse identities while promoting societal stability.

Chapter 2: The Shifting Landscape of Gender Identity and Cultural Change

I. Introduction: A Decade of Transformation

The early 2010s marked a seismic shift in societal attitudes toward gender and identity. What was once a rigid, binary framework of male and female roles evolved into a fluid, complex landscape where identities could no longer be neatly categorized. This chapter examines the cultural, social, and linguistic changes that redefined what it meant to be male, female, or something else entirely, and the role of social media in accelerating these shifts.

II. The Rise of Non-Binary and Fluid Gender Identities

- **A. Expanding the Language of Gender**
    - Before 2010, mainstream discourse on gender was largely binary, centered around traditional male and female categories.
    - Transgender activism introduced concepts like "gender non-conforming," "genderqueer," and other non-binary identities, reshaping public perceptions.
- **B. Social Media's Role in Amplifying New Identities**
    - Platforms like Tumblr and Twitter became incubators for new gender identities, providing marginalized communities with a space to connect and share their experiences.
    - Terms like "agender," "bigender," and "gender-fluid" gained traction, expanding the possibilities of gender expression.
- **C. The Decoupling of Gender Identity from Medical Transition**
    - The traditional notion that one needed medical intervention to change gender gave way to a new standard—self-identification.
    - Gender became more about personal declaration than physical transition, making identity an internal, self-defined state.

III. 2015: A Year of Cultural Overhaul

- **A. The Rise of Cancel Culture**
    - The concept of "cancel culture" emerged, holding individuals, companies, and even fictional characters accountable for perceived offenses.
    - Public figures faced backlash for behaviors and portrayals that had been previously accepted, leading to widespread scrutiny of past actions.
- **B. The Scrutiny of Language and Representation**
    - Language that referenced specific body parts, gender roles, or ethnic stereotypes was suddenly deemed offensive.
    - Hollywood and media industries underwent a reckoning, with portrayals of racial and ethnic characters being harshly criticized as cultural appropriation.
    - Example: Robert Downey Jr.'s portrayal of a black character in *Tropic Thunder* faced renewed criticism.
- **C. The "Canceling" of Beloved Symbols and Characters**

- Beloved icons like Aunt Jemima and Pepe Le Pew were rebranded or removed from popular culture, signaling a shift in what was deemed acceptable.
- These changes were not confined to entertainment; they permeated institutions like the military and academia, where language and traditions were scrutinized and altered.

IV. Language as a Tool of Ideological Change

- **A. Rewriting the Rules of Engagement**
  - Language became a battlefield for ideological change. Terms like "manpower" were replaced with "personnel," and "mother" was substituted with "birthing person" to be more inclusive.
- **B. Institutional Changes in Language and Policy**
  - Even the U.S. military, a traditionally conservative institution, was not immune to this transformation. Gendered titles and ranks came under scrutiny.
  - In corporate and academic settings, employees were encouraged to state their preferred pronouns in professional communications.
- **C. The Weaponization of Language**
  - For some, these changes represented progress; for others, it felt like an imposition, a rewriting of the social contract.
  - Those who struggled to keep up with the evolving lexicon were labeled as ignorant or insensitive, creating a cultural divide.

V. Identity-Based Hiring and Education: The Rise of Affirmative Action 2.0

- **A. From Merit to Identity: A New Hiring Paradigm**
  - By 2015, identity-based hiring practices took precedence over traditional measures of merit. Race, gender, and sexual orientation became key factors in hiring and admissions.
- **B. Unintended Consequences of Identity-Based Evaluation**
  - A new form of "leveling the playing field" emerged, but it sometimes produced paradoxical outcomes.
  - Example: A biracial applicant was initially rejected from a prestigious university, only to be accepted on reapplication when she identified solely as Black.
- **C. The Debate Over Diversity vs. Quality**
  - Supporters saw these changes as necessary to counterbalance systemic discrimination. Critics argued that prioritizing identity over merit could undermine productivity and excellence.
  - The broader impact: Did this emphasis on representation improve outcomes, or did it dilute the focus on qualifications and potential?

VI. The Evolution of LGBTQ+ Rights and the Expansion of Pride

- **A. From Gay Rights to a Spectrum of Identities**
  - The LGBTQ+ movement expanded beyond the original fight for gay and lesbian rights to include a spectrum of identities, practices, and expressions.
- **B. The Controversial Expansion of Pride Celebrations**
  - Pride parades, once focused on visibility and acceptance, began to include displays that many found provocative or inappropriate for public spaces.

- The inclusion of BDSM, fetish demonstrations, and other explicit expressions led to questions about the appropriateness of these spaces for families and children.
- **C. The Shift from Rights to Exhibitionism**
  - What began as a fight for inclusion and equality morphed into a broader celebration of diverse—and sometimes controversial—identities.
  - This shift mirrored the expansion of woke ideology, where inclusivity stretched to encompass practices that blurred the lines of public decency and acceptance.

VII. A Shifting Landscape: The Impact on Language, Culture, and Society

- **A. The Consequences of Ideological Shifts**
  - These cultural changes were not isolated; they were visible manifestations of deeper shifts redefining gender, identity, and social norms.
- **B. The Intersection of Gender, Identity, and Ideology**
  - As woke ideology permeated language, hiring, education, and public celebrations, society found itself grappling with a new set of norms.
- **C. Polarization and Backlash: The Cultural Divide**
  - By 2020, these shifts had created a stark divide between those who embraced the new norms and those who felt alienated or threatened by them.
  - The rapid pace of change left many feeling confused and uncertain about their place in an evolving landscape.

VIII. Conclusion: A New Understanding of Identity in the 21st Century

- **A. The Ongoing Evolution of Gender and Identity**
  - The redefinition of identity is still unfolding, with new terms, practices, and norms emerging regularly.
- **B. The Future of Inclusivity and Social Change**
  - As society continues to redefine what it means to be inclusive, the question remains: Can we create a truly inclusive society without alienating those who struggle to adapt?
- **C. A Call for Balance and Understanding**
  - To navigate this shifting landscape, a balanced approach that considers both inclusivity and stability is crucial.
  - The goal should be to respect diverse identities without sacrificing the social cohesion that allows different groups to coexist.

Chapter 3: How Social Media Amplified Woke Ideology - Reader Objectives

1. **Understand the Role of Social Media in Shaping Ideologies:**
   - Learn how social media has transformed fringe beliefs and niche social movements into mainstream discussions.
   - Examine how platforms like Twitter, Facebook, and TikTok have given unprecedented power to social movements, often distorting original intentions.
2. **Explore the Impact of Algorithms on Ideological Narratives:**
   - Gain insight into how social media algorithms prioritize content that provokes strong emotional reactions, thereby amplifying extreme viewpoints.
   - Understand the feedback loop created by likes, shares, and comments that escalate binary narratives, fueling polarization.
3. **Assess the Influence of Influencers and Activists:**
   - Discover the evolution of influencers and activists from grassroots organizers to digital powerhouses with the ability to shape public opinion.
   - Analyze how the need for visibility and engagement turns genuine advocacy into performance, pushing moderate positions toward more radical stances.
4. **Evaluate the Formation of Echo Chambers and Their Impact:**
   - Learn how algorithms create echo chambers that isolate individuals from differing perspectives, leading to a distorted sense of consensus.
   - Explore the consequences for parents navigating complex issues like gender identity when they are only exposed to one-sided viewpoints.
5. **Recognize the Consequences of Turning Children into Political Symbols:**
   - Identify how social media turns children into symbols for ideological battles, leading to intense pressure and unrealistic expectations on young individuals.
   - Analyze the real-world impact on children and parents when public narratives shape identity more than personal experiences.
6. **Examine Social Media's Role in Medicalization:**
   - Discover how stories of children coming out as transgender on social media can pressure parents into pursuing medical interventions prematurely.
   - Evaluate the role of clinics and pharmaceutical companies in intersecting with ideological movements, potentially prioritizing inclusivity over careful evaluation.
7. **Understand the Suppression of Cautious Voices:**
   - Learn how balanced and cautious voices are marginalized in favor of more radical stances, creating a skewed narrative that influences parental decisions.
   - Reflect on the consequences of this suppression and its impact on the broader discussion around children's well-being.
8. **Develop a Framework for Digital Responsibility:**
   - Understand the need for digital responsibility when addressing complex identity issues, recognizing the double-edged nature of social media's power.
   - Gain strategies for fostering thoughtful and inclusive conversations that prioritize the well-being of individuals over ideological agendas.

Chapter 3: How Social Media Amplified Woke Ideology

I. Introduction: The Digital Megaphone—From Margins to Mainstream

Social media has become one of the most powerful platforms for spreading ideas, shaping movements, and turning fringe beliefs into mainstream narratives. In the past, social justice movements relied heavily on grassroots organizing, community gatherings, and occasional media coverage to gain traction. However, the rise of platforms like Twitter, Facebook, and TikTok has enabled even the most niche ideologies to reach millions in a matter of hours.

This transformation has given unprecedented power to social movements, but it has also accelerated the spread of polarizing viewpoints, often distorting their original intentions. Nowhere is this phenomenon more evident than in the evolution of woke ideology. Once rooted in African American culture as a call to stay vigilant against social injustices, "woke" has rapidly evolved. By the 2010s, it expanded to encompass a range of issues such as gender identity, LGBTQ+ rights, and sexual autonomy—often treated with less nuance in the fast-paced, attention-driven world of social media.

II. Algorithms and the Weaponization of Outrage

- **A. The Role of Algorithms in Content Prioritization** Social media algorithms are designed to maximize user engagement by showing content that elicits strong emotional responses. This algorithmic prioritization is not neutral; it inherently favors posts that provoke outrage, shock, or intense agreement.
- **B. The Creation of a Feedback Loop** Content that generates high engagement—through likes, comments, and shares—is more likely to be seen by a broader audience, creating a feedback loop that rewards extreme narratives. In the context of woke ideology, this has led to a rapid escalation of discussions that might have once been confined to academic circles.
- **C. From Complex Discussions to Binary Narratives** Debates about gender, sexuality, and identity, which are often nuanced and complex, are distilled into bite-sized, incendiary content tailor-made for virality. Hashtags like #TransRightsAreHumanRights and #ProtectTransKids began trending, often framing these issues in stark moral terms, where dissenting voices are labeled as oppressive or bigoted.

III. From Awareness to Orthodoxy: The Role of Influencers and Activists

- **A. The Rise of Influencer Activism** Platforms like Instagram, TikTok, and YouTube have democratized who can become a public figure, allowing anyone with an internet connection to amass a following. Influencers and activists have used these platforms to advocate for marginalized groups and bring attention to critical issues such as gender dysphoria and non-binary identities.

- **B. Advocacy Turned Performance** The relentless need to produce content, gain followers, and maintain visibility often turns genuine advocacy into performance. This dynamic rewards the loudest and most radical voices, pushing influencers to adopt more extreme positions over time.
- **C. Escalation of Ideological Positions** What starts as moderate advocacy can quickly escalate. For example, advocating for trans adults' right to healthcare can transform into promoting immediate medical interventions for children. Social media's demand for constant content drives this escalation, leaving little room for moderate or measured viewpoints.

IV. Creating Echo Chambers: How Social Media Shapes Perception

- **A. The Formation of Echo Chambers** Algorithms personalize content based on user preferences, showing people more of what they already agree with and less of what they might disagree with. This creates a distorted reality where it appears that everyone shares similar opinions, even if those views are far from universal.
- **B. The Impact on Parental Decision-Making** For parents navigating complex issues like gender identity, echo chambers can be especially powerful. A mother who posts about her child's non-traditional preferences may receive overwhelming encouragement to affirm her child's identity, isolating her from voices that advocate for caution.
- **C. The Consequences of Rapid Reinforcement** Within days, a concerned parent might shift from curiosity to becoming an advocate for early medical interventions. The rapid reinforcement of certain ideologies can lead to hasty decisions without fully understanding long-term consequences. Doubt is framed as bigotry, and caution is seen as harm, creating immense pressure to act quickly.

V. Turning Children into Political Symbols

- **A. The Use of Children as Symbols in Ideological Battles** One of the most troubling aspects of social media's amplification of woke ideology is how it has turned children into symbols. Stories of young children coming out as transgender or non-binary are often shared with fervor, celebrating them as heroes of a cultural narrative.
- **B. The Pressure of Public Expectation on Children's Identity** Behind every viral story is a real child who may not fully understand the attention they're receiving or the implications of the narrative constructed around them. Social media often shapes children's identities more by online expectations than by their own experiences.
- **C. The Impact of Instant Virality on Parents and Children** Any hesitation or pushback from parents is met with immediate backlash, labeling them as unsupportive or abusive. This creates a climate where the focus shifts from what's best for the child to what will gain the most social approval.

VI. The Role of Social Media in Medicalization

- **A. The Influence on Parental Actions** When children are celebrated online for coming out as transgender, parents may feel compelled to pursue medical interventions like

hormone therapy or puberty blockers. These stories are often presented as positive, life-affirming decisions, with little discussion of potential risks.
- **B. The Intersection of Ideology and Industry** Clinics and pharmaceutical companies offering gender-affirming care for minors have seen increased demand, driven in part by social media visibility. This intersection between ideology and profit raises concerns about whether inclusivity is sometimes prioritized over caution and thorough evaluation.
- **C. The Suppression of Cautious Voices** Activists and influencers advocating for medical interventions are elevated, while those recommending a more cautious approach are marginalized or labeled as harmful. This suppression of balanced voices creates a skewed narrative that impacts parents' decisions.

VII. Conclusion: A Call for Digital Responsibility

Social media has undeniably played a crucial role in amplifying woke ideology, bringing attention to issues of identity and inclusivity. However, its power can be a double-edged sword. When used responsibly, it can foster understanding and create supportive communities. But when wielded recklessly, it can distort reality, pressure parents into making hasty decisions, and turn children into symbols rather than individuals.

Navigating the complexities of identity in the digital age requires care, nuance, and a deep awareness of social media's influence. Only by fostering thoughtful conversations can we ensure that the voices being amplified seek to protect and uplift, rather than exploit and divide.

Chapter 4: Narcissism in the Digital Age - Reader Objectives

1. **Understand Narcissism and Its Manifestations in Modern Parenting:**
    - Gain insight into the definition and characteristics of Narcissistic Personality Disorder (NPD) and how these traits translate into parenting dynamics.
    - Learn how digital platforms have created new avenues for narcissistic behavior, using children as props for social validation and public admiration.
2. **Explore How Social Media Amplifies Narcissistic Behavior:**
    - Discover how the constant cycle of validation—through likes, comments, and shares—reinforces narcissistic tendencies in parents.
    - Assess how the need for public approval can overshadow a child's needs and personal development, turning children into symbols of parental achievement.
3. **Analyze the Relationship Between Narcissistic Parenting and Münchausen by Proxy:**
    - Learn about Münchausen Syndrome by Proxy (MSBP) and the parallels it shares with narcissistic parenting in the digital age.
    - Understand how some parents may manipulate or fabricate aspects of a child's identity to gain sympathy and admiration, mirroring traditional MSBP patterns.
4. **Examine the Role of Validation in Reinforcing Harmful Parenting Dynamics:**
    - Understand the difference between healthy and toxic validation and how social media can distort a parent's perception of what is truly beneficial for their child.
    - Analyze how children, naturally inclined to seek parental approval, may be pressured into maintaining identities that are not authentic to them.
5. **Identify Signs of Manipulation and Control in Ideological Parenting:**
    - Study real-world examples, such as the case of parental manipulation in New York City, to see how some parents use identity narratives as tools of power and control.
    - Recognize how ideological motivations can lead to decisions that disregard a child's well-being in favor of maintaining a public image.
6. **Understand Ideological Münchausen by Proxy:**
    - Learn how a new form of MSBP—driven by ideological motivations—has emerged, where parents push radical narratives to gain validation as progressive advocates.
    - Explore how social media echo chambers reinforce these behaviors, pushing parents to make increasingly harmful decisions.
7. **Assess the Long-Term Consequences of Parental Narcissism:**
    - Examine the impact on children's identity development, particularly when pressured to conform to public narratives that don't align with their true selves.
    - Understand how the rise of detransitioners is a cautionary example of the potential lifelong effects of parental manipulation and social media's influence.
8. **Develop a Framework for Responsible and Balanced Parenting:**
    - Learn to identify the difference between genuine support and exploitation disguised as advocacy.
    - Gain strategies for encouraging responsible parenting that respects a child's autonomy, prioritizes their emotional and psychological health, and resists the temptation to perform for an audience.

Chapter 4: Narcissism in the Digital Age

I. Introduction: Understanding Narcissism in Modern Parenting

This chapter explores the intersection of narcissism and parenting, with a focus on how digital platforms have transformed parental narcissism into a public performance. It examines how social media has facilitated new forms of narcissistic behavior, drawing parallels between traditional narcissistic traits and the current trend of using children to gain social validation and approval.

II. Defining Narcissism and Its Manifestations

- **A. Narcissistic Personality Disorder (NPD)**
  - According to the Mayo Clinic, Narcissistic Personality Disorder (NPD) is characterized by:
    - An inflated sense of self-importance.
    - A constant need for admiration and attention.
    - A lack of empathy for others.
  - Beneath the façade of confidence lies deep insecurity, making narcissistic individuals highly sensitive to criticism.
- **B. The Dangers of Narcissism in Parenting**
  - Narcissistic parents tend to prioritize their ego and self-image above the needs of their children.
  - This dynamic creates an environment where the child's well-being is secondary to maintaining the parent's narrative of perfection.
  - Criticism or differing perspectives are often met with hostility, making it difficult for others to intervene or offer guidance.

III. The Role of Validation in Reinforcing Behavior

- **A. How Validation Shapes Behavior**
  - Validation is a powerful psychological tool that reinforces behavior in both children and adults.
  - Whether it's praise, attention, or social reinforcement, repeated validation for specific behaviors encourages those behaviors to continue and often amplifies them.
- **B. The Cycle of Social Media Validation**
  - Social media platforms such as Instagram and TikTok use likes, shares, and comments as instant rewards for content creation, reinforcing the desire to seek attention.
  - This validation loop can make narcissistic tendencies more pronounced, particularly in parents who receive positive feedback for sharing details about their children's lives.
- **C. Narcissistic Parenting and Social Media**
  - Narcissistic parents might present their children in ways that draw praise and admiration, often using them as extensions of their own image.

- When parents receive praise for a child's unconventional identity or behavior, it reinforces the desire to continue showcasing the child in that way, regardless of whether it benefits the child.

IV. Linking Narcissism and Münchausen by Proxy

- **A. Understanding Münchausen Syndrome by Proxy (MSBP)**
  - MSBP is a disorder in which a caregiver fabricates or induces illness in a child to gain attention and sympathy.
  - The caregiver's primary focus is on being seen as a dedicated and caring parent, even if it means causing harm to the child.
- **B. Parallels with Narcissistic Parenting**
  - Narcissistic parents may not induce physical illness, but they may manipulate or influence their child's identity to align with a narrative that brings them attention.
  - In both NPD and MSBP, the child's needs are secondary to the parent's emotional or psychological cravings.
- **C. The Evolution of Münchausen by Proxy in the Digital Age**
  - With the rise of social media, some parents exaggerate or fabricate aspects of their child's identity—such as gender dysphoria—to gain admiration for being a "progressive" or "brave" parent.
  - This dynamic is magnified on platforms where parents receive immediate praise and validation, making it difficult to distinguish genuine support from manipulative behavior.

V. The Role of Validation in Parenting Dynamics

- **A. Positive and Negative Forms of Validation**
  - Healthy validation can reinforce positive behaviors and foster creativity, strengthening the parent-child relationship.
  - However, when validation is sought at the expense of the child's autonomy or well-being, it becomes toxic.
- **B. When Parental Validation Turns Harmful**
  - If a parent's need for validation leads them to pressure the child into maintaining a specific identity or behavior, it can have long-term emotional consequences.
  - Children naturally want to please their parents, making them susceptible to internalizing expectations that may not align with their true selves.

VI. Manipulation and Control: When Parenting Crosses the Line

- **A. Case Study: Parental Manipulation in New York City**
  - After a separation, a mother coerced her child into identifying as a different gender. Despite the child's initial resistance, the mother proceeded with hormone treatments, asserting that it was in the child's best interest.
  - The father's objections were dismissed, and the child became a pawn in a larger power struggle between the parents.
- **B. Ideological Narratives as Tools of Manipulation**
  - The parent's need for validation and control overshadowed the child's autonomy, leading to irreversible decisions that disregarded the child's well-being.

VII. Ideological Münchausen by Proxy: A New Form of Child Exploitation

- **A. The Intersection of Narcissism and Ideology**
    - Ideological Münchausen by Proxy occurs when parents use their children to fulfill a narrative that aligns with broader social or political ideologies.
    - The child's well-being is sacrificed to maintain the parent's image as a "brave" advocate for progressive ideals.
- **B. The Role of Social Media Echo Chambers**
    - Echo chambers validate extreme narratives, pushing parents to embrace more radical actions at the expense of the child's emotional health.
    - The more extreme the narrative, the more praise and validation the parent receives, creating a cycle that perpetuates harmful behaviors.
- **C. Recognizing Ideological Münchausen by Proxy**
    - This new form of MSBP is particularly insidious because it often masquerades as progressive parenting. Identifying this behavior requires a careful analysis of the parent's motivations and the impact on the child.

VIII. The Long-Term Consequences of Parental Narcissism

- **A. Impact on Children's Identity Development**
    - Children subjected to narcissistic parenting may struggle with their sense of self, feeling pressured to conform to identities that do not reflect their authentic selves.
- **B. The Rise of Detransitioners**
    - The experiences of detransitioners highlight the dangers of making irreversible decisions based on external validation rather than genuine self-discovery.
    - These stories call for a more cautious and patient approach to children's identity development.

IX. Conclusion: Safeguarding Children's Emotional and Psychological Health

- **A. Recognizing Patterns of Narcissistic and Ideological Parenting**
    - Society must be vigilant in distinguishing between genuine support and exploitation disguised as advocacy.
    - Identifying these patterns is crucial for protecting children from being used as tools for validation.
- **B. Encouraging Balanced and Responsible Parenting**
    - True support respects a child's autonomy and prioritizes their well-being over the parent's need for social approval.
    - Parents must celebrate their child's individuality without using them to gain social clout or validation.
- **C. A Call for Digital Responsibility in Parenting**
    - In the digital age, responsible parenting means resisting the temptation to perform for an audience and focusing on nurturing the child's authentic self.

Chapter 5: The Story of Leane and the Disturbing Trend of Ideological Parenting - Reader Objectives

1. **Understand the Concerns Around Premature Identity Labeling in Children:**
    - Learn about the developmental stages of childhood identity exploration and why interpreting temporary behavior as a fixed identity can be problematic.
    - Gain insight into how cases like Leane's, where a parent publicly declared their toddler as transgender, raise critical questions about the capacity of young children to understand complex concepts such as gender identity.
2. **Explore the Risks of Confusing Playful Exploration with Permanent Identity:**
    - Understand the distinction between normal childhood role-play and permanent identity markers.
    - Examine how some parents might misinterpret playful behaviors as indicators of a child's true gender identity, potentially leading to rushed social or medical interventions.
3. **Analyze the Influence of Social Media and Ideological Echo Chambers:**
    - Investigate how social media platforms act as breeding grounds for extreme parenting narratives, where validation from like-minded communities can push parents to escalate their decisions.
    - Learn about the dangers of echo chambers that reward radical ideas, creating a pressure cooker environment for parents to follow similar paths.
4. **Evaluate the Impact of Pharmaceutical and Corporate Interests:**
    - Discover how pharmaceutical companies have a vested interest in promoting childhood medical transitions, contributing to a profit-driven agenda that intersects with ideological narratives.
    - Assess the growth of the childhood transition industry and the implications for children's long-term health and well-being.
5. **Use Metaphors to Understand the Long-Term Consequences of Premature Identity Affirmation:**
    - Reflect on the metaphor of "The Boy Who Identified as a Vulture" to comprehend the risks of affirming temporary identities without sufficient consideration.
    - Understand the potential for lifelong confusion and alienation when external reinforcement solidifies a fleeting childhood exploration into a fixed identity.
6. **Examine the Concept of Ideological Münchausen by Proxy:**
    - Delve into the idea of Ideological Münchausen by Proxy, where parents may use their child's identity to fulfill their own need for social status and validation.
    - Analyze how this new form of child exploitation leverages ideological narratives for short-term social gain, often at the expense of the child's future well-being.
7. **Identify the Hypocrisy in Ideological Narratives:**
    - Explore how adults who promote extreme identity affirmations in children often have double standards—they advocate for children to adopt these identities while likely rejecting these same behaviors in their adult relationships.
    - Understand the implications of this hypocrisy for the children who are shaped by these narratives.
8. **Highlight the Need for Caution and Responsibility in Parenting:**

- Emphasize the importance of patience and caution when it comes to affirming identities in children.
- Advocate for prioritizing the child's long-term well-being over the parent's short-term need for validation or praise.

9. **Develop Strategies to Avoid Ideological Parenting:**
    - Gain tools to recognize when a parent's motivations might be driven by external validation rather than the child's best interests.
    - Learn how to create a balanced approach to child development that respects the child's natural growth and allows them to explore without imposing fixed identities or irreversible decisions.

Chapter 5: The Story of Leane and the Disturbing Trend of Ideological Parenting

I. Introduction: Leane's Controversial Story

Leane made headlines by asserting that her 2-year-old son identified as a girl. Her story sparked intense debate, as it raised critical questions about the capacity of very young children to understand complex concepts like gender identity. Toddlers often mimic traits they see in others and engage in playful exploration—identifying with fictional characters or pretending to be animals. However, such behaviors are part of normal childhood development, not indicators of a fixed identity.

What made Leane's case particularly alarming was her later suggestion that she supported surgical interventions for young children to "align" their bodies with their perceived identities. This stance is deeply concerning, as no child at the age of two is capable of making a life-altering decision that involves irreversible procedures. The ethical, medical, and psychological implications of pushing a child toward such measures border on abuse.

II. Phases vs. Permanent Changes: A Child's Natural Exploration

- **A. Children's Developmental Phases**
    - Children naturally experiment with different identities and roles as a way of learning about themselves and the world.
    - A child might pretend to be a superhero one day and a dragon the next. This is a normal part of exploration, not a sign of a deep-seated identity that should be medically or socially affirmed.
- **B. Misinterpreting Playful Behavior as a Permanent Identity**
    - When a parent like Leane interprets a toddler's temporary behavior as a definitive statement of gender identity, it raises concerns about whose needs are really being met.
    - Is the focus on the child's genuine interests, or is it on the parent's desire for validation and recognition?
- **C. The Role of Parental Desire for Attention and Social Standing**
    - Parents who push these narratives often gain significant social attention and admiration, especially within certain circles that celebrate "progressive" parenting.
    - It becomes challenging to determine whether they are acting out of genuine concern for their child or being driven by a need for attention and social approval.

III. The Role of Social Media and Ideological Echo Chambers

- **A. The Impact of Social Media on Ideological Narratives**
    - Leane's story is a prime example of how social media has become a breeding ground for radical parenting narratives.
    - Once shared online, her story attracted a significant following of like-minded individuals who praised her for her "courage" and "openness."

- **B. The Validation Trap: Echo Chambers and Social Pressure**
    - The more extreme or provocative the narrative, the more attention it receives, creating an echo chamber where even the most radical ideas—like supporting surgical interventions for toddlers—are encouraged.
    - This creates a space where parents feel pressured to showcase similar experiences, leading to increasingly radicalized decisions.

IV. From Phases to Permanent Consequences: Ignoring the Child's Natural Growth

- **A. Stories of Childhood Phases and Natural Development**
    - Many individuals have shared stories of how they went through phases as children—phases they are grateful were not medically or socially enforced.
    - A common theme emerges: children, especially young ones, are in a constant state of exploration. They might express interests that do not align with their adult identities, but this does not necessitate immediate, irreversible interventions.
- **B. The Risk of Enforcing Identities Based on Fleeting Interests**
    - Imposing an identity on a child based on a temporary interest disregards the natural developmental process.
    - For example, a tomboyish girl may grow up to embrace her femininity, just as boys who briefly showed interest in typically "girlish" activities often go on to live traditionally masculine lives.

V. Pharmaceutical Influence and the Corporate Agenda

- **A. The Role of Pharmaceutical Companies**
    - This issue is not limited to individual parents but has become intertwined with a larger, profit-driven agenda.
    - Pharmaceutical companies have a vested interest in pushing gender-affirming drugs and treatments, as these interventions often require lifelong medical support.
- **B. The Growth of the Childhood Transition Industry**
    - There is a growing industry around childhood transitions, with children being medicalized at younger and younger ages.
    - Parents who may already have narcissistic or attention-seeking tendencies become unwitting participants in a system that prioritizes profit over the well-being of children.

VI. A Metaphor for Today: The Boy Who Identified as a Vulture

- **A. Summary of the Story**
    - In the metaphorical tale, a young boy insists he is a vulture, doing everything he can to embody this identity. But without external encouragement or validation, he eventually realizes that he is not a vulture—he was simply exploring, as children do.
- **B. What Would Happen in Today's World?**
    - If this story took place today, it's easy to imagine a different outcome: teachers and parents affirming his vulture identity, making accommodations for him to "live" as a bird.

- By the time he reaches adulthood, he may have lost sight of who he truly is, facing alienation, loneliness, and confusion.
- **C. The Moral of the Story**
  - The lack of external reinforcement allowed him to return to his true self. The story highlights the dangers of affirming temporary identities without giving children the space to naturally develop and discover themselves.

VII. Ideological Parenting: A Risky Path for the Child

- **A. Children as Unwilling Participants**
  - The most tragic aspect of Leane's story and similar cases is that the child becomes an unwilling participant in the parent's quest for attention and approval.
  - Teachers and online supporters may cheer the parent on, but none of them will be there when the child reaches adulthood, struggling with an identity that may have been more a product of manipulation than self-discovery.
- **B. Hypocrisy in Ideological Narratives**
  - As adults, these same teachers, social media supporters, and ideologically driven parents would likely never date or marry someone who identifies as an animal or who has been shaped by such extreme interventions.
  - They would view such behavior as odd or a sign of instability, yet they encourage children to adopt these identities, knowing full well it may doom them to a life of social isolation and rejection.
- **C. Ideological Münchausen by Proxy: A New Form of Child Exploitation**
  - This hypocritical double standard reveals a disturbing truth: for some parents, the child's future well-being is sacrificed for short-term praise and social status.
  - This makes Ideological Münchausen by Proxy a far more dangerous and insidious form of child exploitation.

VIII. Conclusion: The Need for Caution and Responsibility

- The exploitation of children in pursuit of social validation is a growing concern in modern parenting.
- As society navigates these complex issues, it is crucial to prioritize children's well-being over parents' need for attention.
- True advocacy means giving children space to explore without imposing identities or making irreversible decisions based on fleeting interests.

Chapter 6: Stories of Regret: Children Who Detransitioned and Feel Manipulated by Their Parents - Reader Objectives

1. **Understand the Complexity of Gender Transitions for Minors:**
    - Gain insight into the lesser-known experiences of detransitioners—individuals who transitioned at a young age but later regretted their decision.
    - Explore why some children who transition feel misled or manipulated by their parents, educators, or medical professionals, and why they ultimately decide to revert to their original gender identity.
2. **Recognize the Influence of Social Media and Online Communities:**
    - Learn how social media platforms and peer groups shape young people's perceptions of gender identity and the pressure they create for immediate medical interventions.
    - Understand the power of online communities and echo chambers in glamorizing transitioning, often sidelining cautious or balanced perspectives.
3. **Analyze Real-Life Detransition Stories:**
    - Delve into the stories of prominent detransitioners like Chloe Cole and Helena Kerschner to understand their experiences, regrets, and advocacy for more thoughtful approaches to gender identity.
    - Assess how early transitions, influenced by social or parental factors, have led to lasting physical, emotional, and psychological consequences for these individuals.
4. **Examine the Role of Medical Professionals and Experts:**
    - Review the concerns of researchers like Dr. Lisa Littman, Dr. Erica Anderson, and Marcus Evans, who have called for a more measured, individualized approach to supporting gender-diverse youth.
    - Understand the arguments against rapid medicalization, including the need to explore underlying psychological issues and social influences before making life-altering decisions.
5. **Identify the Role of Parents and Caregivers in These Narratives:**
    - Explore how parents and caregivers, often acting out of a desire to be supportive, can sometimes unwittingly push children toward transitions without fully considering the long-term implications.
    - Learn strategies for parents to balance support and caution, prioritizing their child's long-term mental and emotional health over short-term affirmation.
6. **Evaluate the Need for Comprehensive Mental Health Support:**
    - Understand the importance of providing robust mental health resources for minors experiencing gender dysphoria, focusing on exploration and understanding rather than rushing into medical interventions.
    - Consider how a holistic, mental health-first approach can help children navigate their identities without the pressure of irreversible changes.
7. **Recognize the Impact of Pharmaceutical and Corporate Interests:**
    - Analyze how the intersection of pharmaceutical interests and ideological narratives can contribute to the rise of early childhood transitions, often prioritizing profit over careful patient care.
    - Assess the potential consequences of a profit-driven industry that may inadvertently exploit vulnerable youth.
8. **Reflect on the Societal and Ethical Implications:**

- Learn about the ethical and societal concerns surrounding the medicalization of children and adolescents, particularly in cases where rapid intervention is encouraged without sufficient evaluation.
- Consider the need for a more balanced approach that incorporates the voices of those who have detransitioned, ensuring their experiences inform future policies and practices.

9. **Emphasize the Importance of Listening to Detransitioners:**
   - Understand why it is critical to include detransitioners' voices in the broader conversation around gender identity and childhood transitions.
   - Reflect on how their experiences can serve as cautionary tales, urging society to adopt a more nuanced and cautious approach that truly prioritizes the child's well-being.

10. **Promote a Balanced and Cautious Approach to Supporting Gender Identity:**
    - Advocate for a careful, individualized approach that respects the complexities of identity formation in young people.
    - Encourage a shift from immediate affirmation toward comprehensive care that considers the broader social, psychological, and developmental contexts

Chapter 6: Stories of Regret: Children Who Detransitioned and Feel Manipulated by Their Parents

I. Introduction: The Hidden Voices of Detransitioners

The conversation surrounding gender transitions, particularly for minors, often focuses on affirming the identity choices of those exploring their gender. However, a critical aspect that remains underreported is the experience of detransitioners—individuals who regret their transition and choose to revert to their original gender identity. Their voices highlight a sobering reality: not every transition leads to fulfillment, and some individuals feel misled or manipulated into making irreversible changes at a young age.

Due to social and political pressures, these stories are frequently marginalized or downplayed. Yet, they provide a crucial perspective on the complexities of gender identity and the need for a more cautious, thoughtful approach to supporting children's identity development. Understanding the narratives of detransitioners is essential to ensuring that society does not repeat the same mistakes and that future generations are protected from similar harm.

II. The Case of Chloe Cole: A Voice for Detransitioners

Chloe Cole, now 18, has emerged as one of the most prominent detransitioners advocating against early medical interventions. Her story is both heartbreaking and eye-opening.

- **A. Early Transition and Regret**
    - At just 13, Chloe was placed on puberty blockers and started taking testosterone. By 15, she underwent a double mastectomy, a procedure that permanently altered her body.
    - Within a year, Chloe began to regret her decision, realizing that transitioning did not resolve her underlying emotional struggles. She started detransitioning at 16, deeply troubled by the permanence of the changes she had undergone.
- **B. Advocacy and Public Testimony**
    - Chloe now speaks out against performing irreversible medical procedures on minors, arguing that young people lack the maturity to make such life-changing decisions.
    - Her testimony before Congress has been instrumental in influencing legislation in several U.S. states, leading to bans on puberty blockers and surgeries for minors.
    - Chloe's advocacy has become a rallying cry for others who feel similarly misled by the prevailing gender-affirmative approach, urging society to reconsider its rush to medicalize children.

III. Regret and Reversal: Helena Kerschner's Story

Another powerful voice of regret is Helena Kerschner, who, like Chloe, began transitioning at a young age.

- **A. Influence of Online Communities**
    - Influenced by online communities and social media, Helena believed that transitioning would alleviate her discomfort with her body and sense of not fitting in.
    - After starting hormone treatments as a teenager, she soon realized that transitioning did not address her underlying issues.
- **B. Detransitioning and Speaking Out**
    - Helena eventually detransitioned and now speaks out against the pressures young people face in making such drastic decisions.
    - She, along with other detransitioners, highlights the role of social media in glamorizing transitioning, which can create unrealistic expectations for vulnerable teenagers.

IV. The Role of Social Media and Peer Influence in Shaping Identity

A common thread in these stories is the powerful role of social media and online communities in shaping young people's perceptions of gender and identity.

- **A. Social Media as a Driver of Identity Choices**
    - Platforms like TikTok, Instagram, and YouTube often glamorize transitioning and present it as a quick solution to feelings of alienation, loneliness, or self-doubt.
    - These influences can create a sense of urgency for teenagers to transition before fully understanding the lifelong implications.
- **B. Peer Influence and the Need for Acceptance**
    - Adolescents naturally seek acceptance and affirmation from their social circles, making them more susceptible to peer pressure. When transitioning is presented as a pathway to social approval and validation, it becomes difficult for teenagers to resist.
    - The presence of echo chambers on these platforms exacerbates the issue, where any hesitation or skepticism is met with accusations of bigotry, pushing young people toward rapid affirmation without room for nuanced exploration.

V. Expert Concerns and Calls for Caution

Many medical professionals are raising alarms about the rapid escalation of medical interventions for children and teens.

- **A. Dr. Lisa Littman and Rapid-Onset Gender Dysphoria**

- o Dr. Lisa Littman, a researcher who coined the term "rapid-onset gender dysphoria" (ROGD), suggests that social and peer influences play a significant role in a young person's decision to transition.
    - o Her research highlights the need for a thorough examination of the social and psychological factors contributing to a young person's distress before considering medical intervention.
- **B. Dr. Erica Anderson: Caution from Within the Community**
    - o Dr. Erica Anderson, a clinical psychologist and a transgender woman, has cautioned against the hasty affirmation of minors without thorough psychological assessment.
    - o Anderson emphasizes that gender dysphoria in children is often intertwined with other mental health issues that need to be addressed first.
- **C. Marcus Evans: Critique of the Tavistock Gender Clinic**
    - o Marcus Evans, a former clinical director at the UK's Tavistock gender clinic, has spoken out against the trend of rushing young people onto medical pathways without sufficient exploration of underlying issues.
    - o Evans argues that transitioning should not be treated as a "one-size-fits-all" solution, as many young people may be grappling with complex psychological or developmental challenges that require more nuanced care.

VI. A Call for Thoughtful, Individualized Care

The stories of Chloe, Helena, and other detransitioners highlight the need for a more balanced and individualized approach.

- **A. Prioritizing Mental Health Support Over Immediate Medical Intervention**
    - o Minors experiencing gender dysphoria should receive comprehensive mental health support to explore their feelings and identity without rushing into irreversible decisions.
    - o The focus should be on understanding the child's broader psychological and social context, rather than immediately affirming a gender identity through medical means.
- **B. Addressing the Role of Parents and Professionals**
    - o Parents, educators, and medical professionals need to be equipped with the tools and training to navigate these complex situations with care and caution.
    - o The goal should be to support the child's long-term well-being, recognizing that early medicalization may not always be the best option.

VII. Conclusion: Listening to the Voices of Regret

The experiences of detransitioners serve as a critical counterpoint to the dominant narrative surrounding gender transitions. While transitioning can be a positive and affirming experience for many, it is not without its risks—especially for minors. Their stories remind us that when it comes to a child's identity, there are no shortcuts.

Real support involves patience, deep understanding, and a commitment to protecting the long-term well-being of the child, even when it means resisting the pressures of social or ideological trends. By incorporating the voices of detransitioners into the broader conversation, society can move toward a more balanced, cautious approach that truly prioritizes the needs and futures of all young people.

Chapter 7: The State's Role in Gender Ideology - Reader Objectives

1. **Understand the Growing Influence of the State in Family Dynamics:**
   - Recognize the shifting role of the state in shaping not only educational policies but also personal aspects of children's identities.
   - Analyze how the state's involvement in issues of gender identity is redefining traditional family structures and parental authority.
2. **Examine Policies of Secrecy and Their Impact on the Parent-Child Relationship:**
   - Learn about recent policies that allow schools and institutions to withhold information from parents regarding their child's gender identity.
   - Explore the implications of these policies for trust, transparency, and communication between parents and children.
3. **Identify the Legal Consequences for Parents Who Resist:**
   - Discover how parents who object to their child's transition may face investigations, legal battles, or even loss of custody.
   - Understand the severity of criminalizing parental resistance and the consequences this shift has on parental rights and authority.
4. **Assess the Broader Societal Shift Toward State Control:**
   - Explore how these policies are part of a broader trend of expanding state intervention into family life.
   - Analyze the potential long-term effects of the state acting as the primary arbiter of a child's identity and personal development.
5. **Recognize the Role of Media and Institutional Narratives:**
   - Understand how the media and institutions frame parental concerns as extremist or irrational.
   - Evaluate the impact of one-sided media narratives on shaping public perception and policy acceptance.
6. **Draw Historical Parallels and Consider the Risks of Overreach:**
   - Reflect on the historical precedents of state overreach in family affairs and the dangers posed by unchecked government control.
   - Assess whether current policies could pave the way for more intrusive measures that further erode family autonomy.
7. **Consider the Consequences of Incremental Erosion of Parental Rights:**
   - Analyze how small policy shifts are gradually leading to a broader redefinition of the parent-child relationship.
   - Learn about the cumulative impact of these changes on family dynamics, trust, and parental influence.
8. **Promote the Reaffirmation of Parental Roles and Responsibilities:**
   - Advocate for the protection and strengthening of the parent-child relationship as the cornerstone of a child's development.
   - Explore strategies for empowering parents to navigate complex issues around gender identity while respecting their rights and authority.
9. **Encourage a Balanced Approach Between Protecting Children and Respecting Parental Rights:**

- Emphasize the need for policies that protect children's well-being without alienating or sidelining parents.
- Advocate for a collaborative approach that respects the family as the primary source of support and guidance for children.

10. **Highlight the Need for Reclaiming Family Autonomy:**
    - Reflect on the importance of reaffirming the family's role in shaping a child's development, identity, and values.
    - Consider how society can resist further state encroachment and ensure that parents remain central figures in their children's upbringing.

Chapter 7: The State's Role in Gender Ideology

I. Introduction: A New Frontier of Parental Control

The evolving relationship between the state, schools, and parents has become a battleground in the debate over gender identity and children's rights. Traditionally, decisions about raising, educating, and nurturing children were considered the private realm of the family. However, in recent years, governments and institutions have increasingly stepped in, imposing policies that grant children autonomy over significant aspects of their identity—often without parental consent. This trend has sparked growing concerns among parents, who feel their rights and authority are being systematically undermined in favor of state intervention.

What was once unimaginable—a state that decides not just what a child learns, but also who a child should be—has become a plausible reality. The shift from parental to state control raises fundamental questions about the nature of family dynamics and the extent to which the government should influence a child's personal development and identity.

II. Policies of Secrecy: Undermining Parental Authority

One of the most contentious developments has been the adoption of policies allowing schools to withhold information from parents regarding their child's gender identity or social transition. In some jurisdictions, teachers and school administrators are not required to inform parents if a child chooses to adopt a different name, use new pronouns, or present themselves as a different gender while at school. This creates a scenario where children are effectively living two identities—one at home and another at school—without their parents' knowledge.

- **A. The Secrecy Dilemma**
    - Imagine a parent dropping off their child—believing they are sending off "Zach"—only to have the school refer to and treat the child as "Jill" throughout the day without the parent's knowledge.
    - This lack of transparency breeds mistrust and confusion, fundamentally undermining the parent-child relationship.
- **B. Parental Alienation and Legal Implications**
    - Even more alarming is the legal context surrounding these policies. Parents who do discover their child's dual identity and attempt to intervene may find themselves labeled as unsupportive or even accused of emotional abuse.
    - In some regions, this label can trigger investigations by child protective services, further alienating parents and positioning the state as the primary authority in the child's life.

III. Criminalizing Parental Objections: Legal Consequences and Loss of Custody

Recent legislative changes have gone beyond simply keeping parents uninformed—they actively penalize those who disagree with or resist their child's social or medical transition. In certain jurisdictions, a parent's refusal to affirm their child's new identity can lead to severe legal consequences.

- **A. Investigations and Custody Battles**
    - Parents who express concern or request that schools refrain from affirming their child's new identity may be accused of emotional abuse or neglect.
    - Such accusations can initiate a chain reaction, leading to custody battles, legal investigations, and, in extreme cases, loss of parental rights.
- **B. Criminalizing Parental Resistance**
    - In some instances, parents have faced criminal charges for resisting their child's transition, framing them as a threat to their own children's well-being.
    - This marks a profound shift in power dynamics, where parents are no longer seen as the primary advocates for their children's welfare but as potential adversaries to state policy.

IV. Redefining Family: The State's Growing Influence on Parenting

The state's growing involvement in family dynamics is not limited to specific policies or isolated cases—it represents a broader transformation in how the family unit is defined and managed by public institutions.

- **A. Erosion of Parental Rights in Favor of State Intervention**
    - Under the guise of promoting inclusivity and protecting children's rights, the state is increasingly positioning itself as the ultimate arbiter of what is best for a child.
    - This shift is creating a new paradigm where parents are no longer the primary authority in their child's life. Instead, the state's influence expands into more intimate areas, determining not just what children learn but how they see themselves and define their identities.
- **B. A Dangerous Precedent for Family Autonomy**
    - Such policies establish a dangerous precedent, suggesting that the state can override parental authority whenever it deems the parents' views to be contrary to its own.
    - This could lead to even more intrusive measures, where the state not only dictates educational content but also prescribes how children should be socialized and raised at home.

V. Media and Institutional Influence: Shaping Public Perception

The mainstream media and institutional powers have played a crucial role in normalizing these shifts in policy and perception.

- **A. Framing Parental Concerns as Extremist**
    - Many media outlets present these policies as necessary for protecting children's mental health and emotional well-being while downplaying or ignoring the legitimate concerns of parents.
    - This one-sided narrative marginalizes dissenting voices and creates a public perception that parents who question or challenge these policies are irrational, bigoted, or even abusive.
- **B. Institutional Adoption of Ideological Frameworks**
    - Educational institutions, local school boards, and even federal agencies have embraced these ideologies without fully considering their long-term impact.
    - Dissenting parents are often treated not as concerned caregivers but as obstacles to be managed, with schools acting as enforcers of state policy rather than partners in the child's development.

VI. Incremental Erosion of Parental Rights: A Slippery Slope

The erosion of parental rights is often framed as a progressive policy aimed at safeguarding children's well-being. However, by positioning itself as the guardian of children's rights, the state has established a system where it can override parental authority whenever it sees fit.

- **A. Historical Parallels to Authoritarian Regimes**
    - This situation draws uncomfortable comparisons to authoritarian regimes where governments sought to control family life to align with national goals.
    - While we are not at that extreme stage, the foundations being laid today bear an unsettling resemblance to such dystopian scenarios.

VII. A Call for Balance: Reaffirming the Role of the Family

The expanding role of the state in shaping child identity and family dynamics requires a careful reassessment of parental rights and institutional boundaries.

- **A. Protecting the Parent-Child Relationship**
    - It is essential to find a balance that respects a child's evolving understanding of identity while preserving the fundamental rights of parents to guide and nurture their children according to their own values.
- **B. Empowering Families, Not Dividing Them**
    - The goal should be to empower families to navigate these complex issues together, rather than creating policies that drive a wedge between parents and children.

- By reaffirming the role of the family as the primary unit of support and guidance, society can avoid a future where the state holds more power over a child's upbringing than their own parents.

VIII. Conclusion: Reclaiming the Family's Role in Child Development

The ongoing battle over parental rights and state intervention highlights a critical need to reaffirm the family's role as the cornerstone of a child's development. While protecting children is a noble aim, it should not come at the cost of alienating parents or undermining the parent-child relationship.

As the state continues to expand its influence, society must advocate for a balanced approach—one that recognizes the evolving identities of children while ensuring that parents remain central figures in guiding and supporting their development. Only through such a balanced perspective can we safeguard both the rights of children and the integrity of the family.

Chapter 8: Legal Battles and Custody Wars - Reader Objectives

1. **Understand the Legal Complexities in Gender-Related Custody Battles:**
   - Explore how gender identity has introduced new challenges and complexities into traditional custody battles.
   - Recognize the heightened stakes when one parent supports and the other resists gender-affirming treatments for their child.
2. **Analyze the Impact of "Affirmation-Only" Policies on Custody Decisions:**
   - Understand the implications of courts adopting "affirmation-only" policies, where a child's expressed identity is automatically affirmed.
   - Examine how these policies can bias custody outcomes against parents advocating for a cautious or exploratory approach.
3. **Examine High-Profile Cases Illustrating Systemic Bias:**
   - Learn about real-life cases, such as Ted Hudacko and Jeffrey Younger, to see how the legal system is often used to marginalize fathers in gender-related custody disputes.
   - Assess how these cases reflect broader trends and biases within the judicial system.
4. **Explore the Role of Ideology in Shaping Legal Outcomes:**
   - Evaluate how gender ideology is increasingly being used to influence custody decisions, with courts favoring parents who align with progressive gender narratives.
   - Understand how the system's ideological slant can frame one parent as "supportive" and the other as "obstructive," even when both are acting in good faith for their child's well-being.
5. **Identify the Psychological and Developmental Impact on Children:**
   - Consider how removing one parent from a child's life can lead to long-term emotional and developmental issues.
   - Reflect on the importance of maintaining balanced parental involvement in a child's upbringing.
6. **Understand the Legal Precedents and Risks of Criminalizing Parental Resistance:**
   - Explore the consequences of labeling parents as emotionally abusive or harmful for merely questioning the speed or necessity of gender-affirming interventions.
   - Assess how these policies can escalate into legal battles, investigations, or even the loss of custody for concerned parents.
7. **Recognize the Role of Media and Public Opinion in Shaping Legal Perceptions:**
   - Analyze how the mainstream media's portrayal of these cases can create a biased narrative that influences public and judicial opinions.
   - Understand how dissenting voices are often marginalized, complicating efforts to achieve balanced and fair outcomes in custody disputes.
8. **Highlight the Ethical Concerns in Judicial Bias:**
   - Reflect on the ethical implications of judges presiding over cases where they have personal or ideological connections to the issue of gender identity.
   - Consider the need for increased transparency and impartiality to ensure that custody decisions are made in the best interests of the child.
9. **Promote Legal Reforms to Protect Parental Rights:**
   - Advocate for legal reforms that prioritize transparency, impartiality, and balanced evaluations in gender-related custody battles.

- Explore potential policy changes that ensure both parents have a voice in complex decisions about their child's identity and medical treatments.

10. **Encourage a Balanced and Child-Centric Approach in Custody Cases:**
    - Promote a legal framework that considers the long-term well-being of the child rather than short-term ideological victories.
    - Emphasize the need to reaffirm the value of both parents, recognizing that diverse parental perspectives are essential for a child's healthy development.

Chapter 8: Legal Battles and Custody Wars

I. Introduction: The Gender Divide in Custody Battles

Custody battles are never straightforward, but when gender identity becomes a central issue, the stakes are raised even higher. Traditionally, family courts have tended to favor mothers, often viewing them as the primary caregivers. Fathers, on the other hand, have historically faced an uphill battle for equal custody rights, with the legal system often perceiving them as secondary to a child's immediate emotional needs.

In cases where one parent supports a child's social or medical transition and the other opposes it, this existing bias can become even more pronounced, with fathers often bearing the brunt of the system's inclination to favor the affirming parent. This chapter delves into real-life cases where fathers have been stripped of custody rights due to their resistance to gender-affirming treatments, exploring how the legal system has become a battleground for ideological and parental rights.

II. Weaponizing the System: Ideology in Custody Disputes

The growing influence of gender ideology has led to a disturbing trend: the use of the legal system to marginalize one parent—usually the father—based on differing views on gender identity. Fathers who advocate for a cautious or exploratory approach are often framed as unsupportive, emotionally abusive, or even dangerous. This ideological framing has tilted custody battles, pushing many fathers to the periphery of their children's lives.

- **A. The Rise of "Affirmation-Only" Policies**
    - Courts are increasingly adopting an "affirmation-only" approach, where a child's expressed identity is accepted at face value, and any resistance is seen as harmful.
    - This mindset disregards a balanced perspective that takes into account long-term developmental, psychological, and physical implications, particularly in cases involving young children.
- **B. An Unbalanced Battlefield**
    - This ideological shift has given some parents—often the mother—a powerful tool to paint fathers as adversaries, using the courts to enforce their viewpoint and effectively alienate the father from critical decisions.
    - Fathers who object to medical interventions are sometimes labeled as obstructive, risking not only custody but also their reputation and relationship with their child.

III. The Case of Ted Hudacko: A Father's Struggle for Rights

One of the most illustrative cases is that of Ted Hudacko, a father from California who found himself stripped of his parental rights in a highly publicized custody battle.

- **A. A Father's Concerns Dismissed**
    - Ted's wife, Christine, left him in 2019 and soon after claimed that their 15-year-old son, Drew, identified as transgender. Ted was open to understanding his child's identity but raised concerns about the potential long-term health risks associated with puberty blockers and hormone therapy.
    - Despite Ted's valid questions about his child's well-being, the court sided entirely with Christine, awarding her sole custody and decision-making authority over Drew's medical care.
- **B. Judicial Bias and Transparency Issues**
    - Judge Joni Hiramoto, who presided over the case, was later revealed to have a transgender child herself and had publicly advocated for the transition process. This personal connection raised serious ethical concerns about impartiality and bias in her ruling.
    - While the judge's background did not automatically disqualify her, the lack of disclosure fueled suspicions that the outcome may have been influenced by her personal experiences rather than an unbiased assessment of what was in Drew's best interest.
- **C. The Aftermath and Broader Implications**
    - Ted's case is a stark reminder of how fathers can be effectively erased from their children's lives when the legal system prioritizes ideological alignment over balanced parental input. His experience is not unique, as similar cases are emerging across the country, suggesting a troubling trend in family law.

IV. A System Rigged Against Fathers: The Broader Trend

The systemic bias against fathers in custody battles is not new, but the rise of gender identity issues has further deepened this disparity. Courts often view fathers as less nurturing and more resistant to new concepts, such as fluid gender identities. When a father's cautious approach is pitted against a mother's affirming stance, the latter is almost always deemed the more "supportive" option, despite evidence that both parents should be involved in complex decisions about a child's development.

- **A. The Impact on Parental Rights**
    - Fathers are losing not just access to their children but also the right to have a say in life-altering decisions.
    - In some cases, fathers have been subjected to restraining orders or labeled as a threat for merely questioning the speed and intensity of their child's transition process.
- **B. The Psychological Impact on Children**
    - Research consistently shows that children benefit from having both parents actively involved in their upbringing. The absence of a father figure can lead to a range of developmental issues, including emotional instability and behavioral problems.
    - Yet, the courts often disregard these considerations, focusing solely on immediate affirmation rather than long-term outcomes.

V. Real-Life Cases: Fathers on the Losing Side

Beyond Ted Hudacko, there are numerous other cases that illustrate how fathers are being marginalized:

- **Case 1: Jeffrey Younger vs. Anne Georgulas**
    - Jeffrey Younger, a father from Texas, fought to prevent his ex-wife from transitioning their 7-year-old son, James. Younger argued that James did not consistently express a desire to transition and showed comfort in his biological identity when with him.
    - Despite his concerns, the court ruled in favor of the mother, granting her the right to proceed with social transitioning. The case sparked national outrage and brought attention to the fragile state of parental rights.
- **Case 2: The Battle of Rob Hoogland**
    - Rob Hoogland, a Canadian father, was jailed for refusing to comply with court orders that barred him from speaking publicly about his child's medical transition.
    - Hoogland's case raised alarm bells about the extent to which courts could limit parental speech and suppress dissenting opinions in the name of protecting a child's gender identity.

VI. A Call for Reform: Ensuring Fairness in Custody Battles

The legal system's current approach to gender identity in custody battles is deeply flawed, often prioritizing ideology over the child's holistic well-being. Reform is urgently needed to ensure that both parents are treated fairly and that decisions are made in the best interests of the child.

- **A. Prioritizing Transparency and Impartiality**
    - Judges with personal connections or strong views on gender identity should be required to disclose these biases to ensure fair trials.
    - Custody decisions should be based on comprehensive evaluations that consider the child's long-term psychological and developmental needs.
- **B. Protecting Parental Rights and Roles**
    - Both parents should have a say in their child's upbringing, particularly in cases involving irreversible medical interventions.
    - Courts should resist the tendency to equate caution with bigotry, instead fostering a space where diverse viewpoints can be considered in the child's best interest.

VII. Conclusion: Reaffirming the Role of Both Parents

The rising influence of gender ideology in custody battles is reshaping the legal landscape, often leaving fathers on the losing end. As Ted Hudacko and others have shown, the current system can easily be weaponized against one parent, undermining the child's right to have balanced input from both parents. To protect the integrity of the family unit, courts must prioritize a balanced approach, ensuring that neither parent is excluded based on ideological alignment.

By reaffirming the value of both mothers and fathers in a child's life, we can create a more just and supportive legal framework that truly serves the best interests of the child.

Chapter 9: The Intersection of Medicine, Government, and Profit - Reader Objectives

1. **Understand the Influence of Profit Motives in Medical Interventions:**
   - Explore how the pharmaceutical industry has a vested interest in promoting gender-affirming treatments, turning patients into lifelong consumers.
   - Recognize how the introduction of these treatments has created a highly profitable market that incentivizes continuous medical dependency.
2. **Examine the Role of the Government in Shaping Health Policies:**
   - Investigate how government policies have facilitated the expansion of gender-affirming care for minors, sometimes bypassing parental rights.
   - Learn how government endorsement of certain treatments can indirectly promote corporate profit over patient safety and caution.
3. **Analyze the Ethical Dilemmas of Medicine as a Market Commodity:**
   - Consider the ethical implications when patient care intersects with financial incentives, raising questions about whether profit is being prioritized over health.
   - Draw parallels with the opioid crisis as a cautionary tale of the dangers of allowing profit-driven healthcare to dictate patient treatment.
4. **Assess the Financial and Ideological Influence of Pharmaceutical Companies:**
   - Understand how pharmaceutical companies financially support advocacy groups to push for "affirmation-only" models, marginalizing voices that advocate for less invasive treatments.
   - Reflect on how this partnership between ideology and profit skews public perception and limits open, balanced discussions on the risks and benefits of medical interventions.
5. **Explore Real-World Examples and Case Studies:**
   - Delve into real-world scenarios illustrating how financial incentives have shaped healthcare decisions, impacting the way gender dysphoria is treated in children.
   - Examine government contracts and regulatory capture, where regulatory bodies become influenced by the same industries they are supposed to regulate.
6. **Consider the Consequences of Lack of Long-Term Research:**
   - Highlight the risks of promoting treatments that lack comprehensive, long-term research, particularly for children and adolescents.
   - Understand the potential long-term effects of treatments like puberty blockers on bone density, cognitive development, and fertility, which are often downplayed in favor of short-term benefits.
7. **Understand the Concept of Regulatory Capture and Its Implications:**
   - Learn how regulatory bodies like the FDA can be influenced by individuals with ties to pharmaceutical companies, creating conflicts of interest that affect policy-making.
   - Recognize the impact of these dynamics on public health policy, where corporate interests can override patient safety and well-being.
8. **Advocate for Transparency and Reform in Healthcare Policies:**
   - Explore potential policy reforms that prioritize transparency and independent research to protect vulnerable populations from profit-driven healthcare decisions.
   - Support the implementation of stricter disclosure requirements for professionals and policymakers advocating for medical treatments, ensuring accountability.
9. **Reaffirm the Role of Parents in Healthcare Decisions:**

- Discuss the importance of parental involvement in decisions about a child's medical care, advocating for policies that respect family autonomy and parental rights.
- Understand how certain laws sideline parents, making the state or medical professionals the primary decision-makers, and consider the implications for family dynamics.

10. **Promote a Health-First Approach in the Intersection of Medicine and Profit:**
    - Encourage the prioritization of health and patient well-being over financial gain in the development and promotion of treatments.
    - Advocate for a healthcare model that ensures treatments are based on solid evidence, long-term research, and a genuine concern for patient outcomes, not influenced by profit motives.

Chapter 9: The Intersection of Medicine, Government, and Profit

I. Introduction: When Health Becomes a Commodity

The intersection of medicine, government, and profit is a complex and often murky territory where the lines between patient care and financial gain blur. The introduction of third-party interests into healthcare is not a new phenomenon, but it has taken on a troubling new dimension with the rise of childhood gender transitions. This chapter examines how the rapid push for gender-affirming treatments has created a lucrative market for pharmaceutical companies and how government policies have facilitated this trend, sometimes at the expense of children's long-term well-being.

II. The Pharmaceutical Industry's Role in Gender Transitioning

Pharmaceutical companies are key players in the gender transition industry. From puberty blockers and hormone therapies to gender-affirming surgeries, each new patient represents a lifelong consumer for a range of expensive medical treatments. While gender dysphoria is a legitimate mental health condition requiring compassionate care, the aggressive promotion of early medical intervention raises questions about whether the primary driver is health or profit.

- **A. Lifelong Medical Dependency**
    - Puberty blockers, hormone therapies, and surgeries are not just one-time treatments; they often lead to lifelong medical dependency. Once a patient begins transitioning, they typically need continuous medication to maintain their new identity, creating a steady stream of income for pharmaceutical companies.
    - **Example**: A young person starting hormone therapy at 12 will likely require ongoing medical care, including hormone prescriptions, for the rest of their life, making them a profitable long-term customer.
- **B. Financial Incentives and the Expansion of the Market**
    - The financial stakes are immense. As more children are diagnosed with gender dysphoria and begin medical transitions, the demand for hormone therapies and related medical procedures increases exponentially.
    - Pharmaceutical companies have a vested interest in supporting policies and advocacy that promote early intervention, as each new patient can generate substantial long-term revenue.

III. Government Involvement: Policies That Promote Profit Over Caution

Governments play a crucial role in shaping public health policies, but when these policies intersect with powerful corporate interests, conflicts of interest can arise. Policies that promote early medical intervention for gender dysphoria are often framed as necessary for protecting mental health, yet they also serve to legitimize and expand a lucrative market for pharmaceutical companies.

- **A. Government Endorsement and Legitimization**
    - Some lawmakers and regulators who advocate for greater access to gender-affirming care have financial or political ties to pharmaceutical companies. These connections create a feedback loop where government policy is influenced by corporate interests.
    - **Example**: When government health agencies endorse puberty blockers or hormones as "safe and effective" without long-term data, they indirectly promote the use of these drugs, boosting the market.
- **B. Policies That Sideline Parental Rights**
    - In some regions, governments have enacted policies that allow children to receive gender-affirming care without parental consent. While these policies are often justified as protecting children's autonomy, they also serve to undermine parental involvement and push medical interventions at a younger age.
    - **Example**: California's law allowing minors to access hormone therapy without parental consent effectively turns the state into a gatekeeper for these treatments, bypassing family involvement.

IV. The Profit Motive in Medicine: From Treatment to Commodity

The financial incentives for medical institutions and clinics are just as compelling as those for pharmaceutical companies. In the United States, clinics offering gender-affirming care can receive significantly higher reimbursements from insurance companies compared to standard pediatric care. This economic model creates a perverse incentive for doctors to recommend these treatments, even when less invasive options may be more appropriate.

- **A. Clinics and Medical Professionals: The Push for Profit**
    - Medical professionals may unconsciously (or consciously) push for transitioning treatments due to the higher profit margins associated with these procedures. This can lead to situations where treatments are recommended before exploring less invasive alternatives.
    - **Example**: A pediatric clinic specializing in gender-affirming care can charge insurance significantly more for hormone therapies and surgeries than for regular health checkups or counseling sessions.
- **B. The Role of Ideological Advocacy**
    - Ideological advocacy groups often receive funding from pharmaceutical companies to promote "gender-affirming" care as the only ethical approach. This creates a scenario where any dissenting voices—such as those advocating for caution or psychological support first—are drowned out by well-funded campaigns that push a singular narrative.

V. The Ethical Dilemma: Medicine or Market?

When medicine becomes intertwined with ideology and profit, the ethical dilemmas multiply. The promotion of early and aggressive medical interventions for children raises serious ethical concerns about consent, autonomy, and the role of profit in shaping healthcare decisions.

- **A. Profit Over Patient Well-Being?**

- o The aggressive promotion of medical transitions, especially for minors, suggests that financial incentives may be outweighing genuine concerns for patient welfare. The push for rapid intervention is often justified using emotionally charged language, portraying any delay as harmful, even when the long-term risks are not fully understood.
- o **Parallel Example**: The opioid crisis serves as a cautionary tale of what happens when profit-driven healthcare is allowed to run unchecked. Pharmaceutical companies aggressively marketed opioids while downplaying the risks, leading to widespread addiction and a public health disaster.
- **B. Lack of Long-Term Research**
  - o Many of the treatments being recommended lack comprehensive, long-term research, especially for children. Despite this, they are being presented as low-risk solutions, creating a misleading sense of security.
  - o **Example**: Puberty blockers, once described as a "pause button," are now being shown to have potential long-term effects on bone density, cognitive development, and fertility.

VI. Government Contracts and the Influence of Big Pharma

The role of government contracts in the promotion and distribution of these treatments cannot be understated. Government agencies often rely on research and recommendations from the very companies that stand to profit, creating a conflict of interest that skews public health policy.

- **A. Public Funding and Corporate Profit**
  - o When governments contract pharmaceutical companies to supply treatments, such as puberty blockers or hormones, they effectively become partners in the commercialization of these therapies.
  - o **Example**: A single government contract for hormone therapies can be worth millions, making it a lucrative venture for pharmaceutical companies and creating a strong incentive to push for broader access.
- **B. Regulatory Capture: When Companies Set the Rules**
  - o Regulatory bodies, such as the FDA in the United States, are often staffed by individuals who have worked for or have connections to pharmaceutical companies. This "revolving door" phenomenon creates an environment where corporate interests can shape public policy.

VII. A Call for Reform: Protecting Patients Over Profit

To protect children and families from the potentially harmful effects of profit-driven healthcare, a new approach is needed—one that prioritizes patient well-being over financial gain. This will require stronger regulations, greater transparency, and a commitment to long-term research.

- **A. Full Disclosure of Conflicts of Interest**
  - o Any professional or policymaker advocating for these treatments should be required to disclose any financial ties to pharmaceutical companies. Transparency is crucial for building public trust.
- **B. Independent Research and Review**

- o Long-term, independent studies must be prioritized to assess the safety and effectiveness of these treatments for children and adolescents. Funding for this research should come from neutral sources to avoid bias.
- **C. Reaffirming Parental Rights**
  - o Parents must be empowered to make informed decisions about their child's healthcare, without fear of government overreach or manipulation by third-party interests. Policies should ensure that parents are fully involved in these decisions, except in cases of proven abuse or neglect.

VIII. Conclusion: Prioritizing Health Over Profit

The intersection of medicine, government, and profit is fraught with ethical challenges. When profit motives overshadow patient care, vulnerable populations—especially children—are put at risk. It is essential to create a healthcare system that prioritizes health and safety over financial gain, ensuring that treatments are based on solid evidence and genuinely serve the best interests of the patient.

Chapter 10: The Emotional and Psychological Toll - Reader Objectives

1. **Understand the Psychological and Emotional Development of Children and Adolescents:**
    - Learn about the distinct stages of childhood and adolescent development, such as the Pre-operational Stage (Ages 2-7), the Concrete Operational Stage (Ages 7-12), and Adolescent Brain Development (Ages 12-18).
    - Recognize how these developmental stages influence a child's understanding of identity, permanence, and long-term decision-making.
2. **Examine the Limitations of Adolescent Decision-Making:**
    - Understand that the prefrontal cortex, responsible for weighing long-term consequences, does not fully mature until around age 25.
    - Assess why adolescents may not have the cognitive and emotional maturity to comprehend the lifelong implications of medical interventions like hormone therapy or surgery.
3. **Explore the Short- and Long-Term Emotional Impacts of Early Transitions:**
    - Delve into the short-term emotional challenges such as heightened anxiety, social isolation, and identity confusion that children and adolescents may experience when transitioning early.
    - Consider the potential long-term psychological consequences, including regret, depression, and a sense of betrayal as expressed by many detransitioners.
4. **Analyze the Experiences and Stories of Detransitioners:**
    - Gain insight from real-world stories like Chloe Cole, Richie, and others who have detransitioned and now speak out about the emotional toll and regret associated with early transitions.
    - Understand how these voices provide critical perspectives on the hidden costs of transitioning at a young age, challenging the dominant narrative that affirms early interventions as the only solution.
5. **Assess the Role of Social Isolation and Unintended Outcomes:**
    - Learn how early transitioning can lead to social isolation and alienation, making it harder for individuals to find romantic partners and integrate into society.
    - Examine case studies, such as that of Norah Vincent, to understand the harsh social realities of transitioning and the emotional toll it can take when societal acceptance is not forthcoming.
6. **Critically Evaluate the Influence of External Pressures and Emotional Manipulation:**
    - Explore how influencers, activists, and emotional predators can manipulate vulnerable children into making drastic decisions without fully understanding the consequences.
    - Consider the impact of peer pressure, social media, and ideological advocacy in shaping young people's perceptions and pushing them toward irreversible choices.
7. **Discuss the Dangers of Alienation from Family Support Systems:**
    - Understand how some activists encourage children to reject parental guidance, framing familial concern as bigotry, which can lead to estrangement and emotional vulnerability.
    - Reflect on the importance of maintaining open communication and family involvement to support a child's development and well-being.

8. **Identify Safeguards and Standards for Protecting Vulnerable Children:**
    - Advocate for rigorous medical standards and thorough psychological evaluations before considering any irreversible interventions for children and adolescents.
    - Promote the implementation of non-invasive therapeutic approaches and psychological support as the first step in helping children explore their identities.
9. **Promote a Balanced Approach That Prioritizes Long-Term Well-Being:**
    - Emphasize the need for caution, long-term research, and responsible decision-making to ensure that every child makes informed choices without external pressure or ideological influence.
    - Consider policies and practices that prioritize a child's holistic well-being over short-term validation or social approval, ensuring that medical decisions are guided by sound evidence and genuine concern for the child's future.
10. **Encourage Compassion and Responsibility in Addressing Childhood Transitions:**
    - Advocate for a compassionate approach that respects a child's exploration of identity while safeguarding against hasty or irreversible decisions.
    - Promote a framework that prioritizes caution, responsibility, and a commitment to protecting vulnerable children from the emotional and psychological toll of early transitions.

Chapter 10: The Emotional and Psychological Toll

I. Introduction: Childhood Transitions—A Complex Terrain

The decision to transition, particularly at a young age, carries profound emotional and psychological ramifications. Children and adolescents, still in the process of developing their sense of self, may lack the cognitive and emotional maturity to fully understand the long-term consequences of such irreversible choices. While the discourse around gender identity often emphasizes the right to self-determination, it is crucial to explore how early transitions impact mental health and well-being over the long term.

II. Understanding Childhood and Adolescent Psychology

The cognitive and emotional development of children follows a predictable trajectory, with distinct stages that influence how they perceive themselves and the world around them. At each stage, children process identity, autonomy, and permanence in unique ways, making it essential to consider these factors before endorsing life-altering decisions.

- **A. The Developmental Science**
    - **Pre-operational Stage (Ages 2–7)**: During early childhood, children operate primarily through imagination and concrete thinking. They may frequently change identities in play, pretending to be animals, superheroes, or even different genders. However, these changes are not indicative of a fixed sense of self.
    - **Concrete Operational Stage (Ages 7–12)**: As children grow, they begin to develop logical thought but still struggle with abstract concepts. They understand rules and permanence better, but their grasp on complex ideas like gender identity is limited.
    - **Adolescent Brain Development (Ages 12–18)**: Adolescents are more capable of abstract thought but remain highly influenced by social approval and are prone to impulsive decision-making due to the ongoing maturation of the prefrontal cortex, the part of the brain responsible for weighing long-term consequences.
- **B. The Limitations of Adolescent Decision-Making**
    - The prefrontal cortex—the brain's decision-making center—does not fully mature until around age 25. This means that even older teenagers may struggle to foresee the long-term effects of medical interventions like hormone therapy or surgery, making them vulnerable to decisions that may lead to regret.

III. The Emotional Toll of Early Transitions

Early transitions can have a lasting impact on a child's emotional and psychological state. The experiences of those who have detransitioned often reveal a pattern of emotional distress, regret, and a sense of being misled during a vulnerable period of their lives.

- **A. Short-Term Emotional Challenges**

- Children and adolescents who transition early often experience heightened anxiety, social isolation, and identity confusion. While transitioning may initially provide a sense of relief, it can later lead to distress when children are confronted with the realities of irreversible physical changes.
- **Example**: Adolescents who undergo puberty blockers may struggle with their peers' experiences of puberty, feeling left behind and alienated as they fail to go through the same developmental milestones.
- **B. Long-Term Psychological Consequences**
    - The lack of comprehensive long-term studies makes it difficult to predict the full range of psychological impacts, but anecdotal evidence from detransitioners suggests high levels of depression, anxiety, and a deep sense of regret. Detransitioners often report feeling like they were rushed into a decision that permanently altered their lives without fully understanding the consequences.

IV. Stories of Regret: Voices of Detransitioners

Detransitioners provide critical insight into the hidden emotional toll of transitioning at a young age. Their stories reveal how the promise of happiness and relief turned into lifelong struggles with identity, mental health, and a sense of betrayal.

- **A. The Case of Chloe Cole**
    - Chloe began transitioning at age 13 and underwent a double mastectomy by 15. She later realized that her decision was driven by a desire to escape her discomfort rather than a true understanding of her identity. By 16, she regretted her transition and detransitioned. Today, Chloe speaks out against early transitions, advocating for more cautious approaches that prioritize mental health support.
- **B. Richie's Story**
    - Richie was prescribed hormones after only two brief consultations. He now describes himself as a "neutered male" and expresses deep regret over the irreversible surgeries. Richie's experience highlights how some medical professionals are quick to recommend drastic treatments without adequate psychological evaluation.
- **C. The Mother Who Regrets Mastectomy**
    - A woman who detransitioned after undergoing a double mastectomy at age 20 described the anguish she felt when she couldn't breastfeed her child years later. Her story, documented in *Frontiers in Global Women's Health*, reveals the profound and often unanticipated consequences of early surgical interventions.

V. Social Isolation and the Reality of Transitioning

For many, transitioning leads to social isolation and romantic challenges. While the hope is often that transitioning will bring relief and acceptance, the reality can be starkly different.

- **A. The Loneliness of Transition**
    - Transitioning can sometimes result in feelings of alienation, as societal acceptance is not always forthcoming. Trans men and women often struggle to find romantic partners and may face prejudice and discrimination in various social settings.

- **Example**: Norah Vincent, a journalist who lived as a man for a year, ended her life after struggling with the loneliness and emotional toll of her experience. Her story underscores the harsh realities of living as a gender that society may not fully accept.

VI. The Impact of Emotional Manipulation and Ideological Pressure

Young people are particularly vulnerable to external influences from social media, peers, and even well-meaning adults. Emotional predators—individuals who use their platform to push vulnerable children toward drastic decisions—are a growing concern.

- **A. The Role of Influencers and Activists**
    - Influencers like "D. Muveney" (a pseudonym) often glamorize the idea of transitioning, presenting it as a simple, joyous solution to complex identity issues. This portrayal ignores the long-term psychological and social implications, leaving young people ill-equipped to navigate their decisions.
- **B. The Danger of Isolation from Family Support**
    - Many activists encourage children to reject the guidance of their parents, framing any opposition as bigotry. This can lead to estrangement from family support systems, leaving children more vulnerable to manipulation and exploitation.

VII. A Call for Responsibility: Protecting Vulnerable Children

Given the complexity of childhood and adolescent development, it is essential to prioritize caution, psychological support, and parental involvement over irreversible medical interventions. Children should not be placed on paths that could lead to permanent regret and psychological harm without comprehensive, long-term research and a clear understanding of the consequences.

- **A. Implementing Safeguards and Standards**
    - The medical community must adopt rigorous standards for evaluating children with gender dysphoria, ensuring that interventions are based on sound evidence and not ideology or profit motives.
- **B. Encouraging Psychological Support First**
    - Before considering any medical interventions, children should receive thorough psychological evaluations and support to explore their identity in a safe, non-permanent way. Therapy, family counseling, and support groups can provide healthier avenues for self-discovery.

VIII. Conclusion: A Call for Caution and Compassion

The emotional and psychological toll of early transitions is a reality that must be addressed with compassion, responsibility, and a commitment to protecting vulnerable children. Until we can guarantee that every child is making informed, autonomous decisions free from external pressure, the priority must be to proceed with caution, ensuring that long-term well-being is always placed above short-term validation or social approval.

Chapter 11: Stories of Detransitioners - Reader Objectives

1. **Gain an Understanding of Detransition and Its Importance:**
   - Define detransitioning and recognize it as a critical part of the broader discussion on gender identity and childhood transitioning.
   - Understand why detransitioners' experiences matter, particularly in highlighting the complexities and potential risks of early transitioning decisions.
2. **Comprehend the Physical and Physiological Challenges Detransitioners Face:**
   - Learn about the irreversible changes that transitioning can cause, including loss of reproductive ability, permanent physical alterations, and complications from surgeries.
   - Understand the physical struggles detransitioners endure, such as attempting to reverse changes that may only be partially reversible and coping with the consequences of early medical interventions.
3. **Explore the Emotional and Psychological Impact of Detransitioning:**
   - Delve into the profound emotional toll detransitioning can take, including feelings of regret, grief, and betrayal.
   - Consider the identity confusion and social stigma detransitioners face, which often leave them feeling isolated and disconnected from both the transgender and wider communities.
4. **Examine Real-Life Case Studies of Detransitioners:**
   - Gain insights from the lived experiences of detransitioners like Chloe Cole, Richie, and Elizabeth, each of whom provides a unique perspective on the complexities of early transitioning and the consequences they now live with.
   - Understand how their stories illustrate the hidden costs of rushing into gender-affirming treatments without thorough psychological evaluation and support.
5. **Analyze the Lack of Support and Resources for Detransitioners:**
   - Learn about the significant gaps in healthcare and mental health support for detransitioners, including limited access to knowledgeable healthcare providers and inadequate mental health resources.
   - Understand how the medical and mental health communities that once supported their transition are often unprepared or unwilling to assist them in the detransition process, leaving detransitioners feeling abandoned.
6. **Critically Assess the Role of Informed Consent and Psychological Support:**
   - Recognize the importance of comprehensive psychological support and informed consent for anyone considering transitioning, particularly minors.
   - Advocate for a more cautious approach that includes addressing underlying mental health issues and ensuring that decisions are made with a full understanding of the potential consequences.
7. **Consider the Long-Term Implications of Early Transitioning:**
   - Understand the broader implications of early transitions on future well-being, including the emotional toll of regret and the potential for permanent physical changes that cannot be undone.
   - Reflect on how a rush to transition without thorough evaluation can lead to long-term distress, isolation, and a sense of lost identity for those who later decide to detransition.
8. **Advocate for a More Balanced and Compassionate Approach to Gender Identity:**

- Explore the need for a balanced approach that listens to detransitioners' voices, validates their experiences, and uses their stories to inform a more cautious and nuanced policy on gender-affirming care.
- Emphasize the need for policies and practices that prioritize thorough psychological support and comprehensive informed consent, particularly for children and adolescents.

9. **Encourage a Cultural Shift Toward Inclusivity and Understanding:**
    - Promote the importance of creating a safe and inclusive space for detransitioners to share their stories without stigma or judgment.
    - Advocate for a cultural shift that acknowledges the diverse range of experiences within the gender identity community and fosters a compassionate dialogue that respects each individual's journey.

10. **Conclude with a Call to Listen and Learn from Detransitioners:**
    - Highlight that detransitioners' voices should not be marginalized or silenced but rather integrated into the broader conversation on gender identity and transitioning.
    - Encourage readers to approach the issue with empathy and a willingness to learn, ensuring that future decisions about gender-affirming care are made with a comprehensive understanding of all possible outcomes.

Chapter 11: Stories of Detransitioners

I. Introduction: The Hidden Voices of Detransitioners

The stories of detransitioners are among the least discussed but most critical aspects of the conversation surrounding gender identity and childhood transitioning. These individuals, who transitioned at a young age but later regretted the decision, often face significant emotional, physical, and social challenges as they attempt to reverse the changes. Their experiences are a stark reminder that decisions made during adolescence can have lasting and sometimes irreversible consequences. Yet, in a culture that often prioritizes affirmation over caution, detransitioners are frequently marginalized, their voices silenced, and their pain overlooked.

II. Understanding Detransition: What It Means and Why It Matters

Detransitioning is the process of ceasing a gender transition and returning to one's biological sex or original gender identity. For those who detransition, the journey is not just about changing one's appearance or stopping hormone treatments—it's about reclaiming a sense of self that feels true and authentic. The path to detransition is fraught with obstacles, both internal and external, as detransitioners grapple with feelings of regret, betrayal, and confusion, while also dealing with the physical and medical realities of reversing the changes made to their bodies.

III. The Physical and Physiological Challenges of Detransitioning

The physical consequences of transitioning are often permanent or only partially reversible, leaving detransitioners to navigate the aftermath of choices made when they were too young to fully understand the long-term impact.

- **A. Loss of Reproductive Ability**

    One of the most devastating consequences of transitioning is the loss of reproductive health. Puberty blockers, hormone therapy, and surgical interventions can irreversibly damage reproductive organs, leaving many detransitioners infertile. This loss is particularly heart-wrenching for those who, after detransitioning, develop a desire to start a family—a desire that was either not fully considered or dismissed during their transition.

- **B. Irreversible Changes to Physical Appearance**

    Hormone treatments and surgical interventions lead to permanent changes that are not easily undone. For female detransitioners who took testosterone, these changes might include a deeper voice, facial hair, and a more angular bone structure. Similarly, male detransitioners who took estrogen might develop breast tissue and softer facial features. Attempting to reverse these changes can be painful and, in many cases, only partially effective.

- **C. Post-Surgical Complications**

    Detransitioners who have undergone gender-affirming surgeries, such as mastectomies or genital reconstruction, often face additional complications when they decide to revert. These surgeries can result in chronic pain, scar tissue, and loss of sensation, making the detransition process even more physically and emotionally taxing.

IV. Emotional and Psychological Challenges

Beyond the physical difficulties, the emotional and psychological toll of detransitioning is profound. Many detransitioners describe a deep sense of regret, confusion, and betrayal—by medical professionals, by the trans community, and even by themselves.

- **A. Regret, Grief, and Betrayal**

    The most common emotion reported by detransitioners is regret, often accompanied by grief for the person they could have been. This regret is compounded by a sense of betrayal—by the medical professionals who facilitated their transition, by the social communities that encouraged it, and sometimes even by their own families. Many feel that their psychological struggles were overlooked, and that alternative treatments were not considered.

- **B. Identity Confusion**

    After years of identifying as another gender, detransitioners often feel disconnected from both their original and transitioned identities. This leaves many feeling lost, caught between two worlds, and struggling to find a sense of self that resonates with who they are now.

- **C. Social Stigma and Isolation**

    Detransitioners often face stigma from multiple fronts. The trans community may see them as traitors, while the general public may not fully accept them. This dual rejection leads to profound isolation and loneliness, making it difficult for detransitioners to find a supportive community or sense of belonging.

V. Case Studies of Detransitioners: Real Stories, Real Consequences

Personal stories offer powerful insight into the lived experiences of detransitioners. Below are some of the most compelling accounts that highlight the complexity and pain of detransitioning.

- **A. Chloe Cole: A Young Life Irrevocably Changed**

    Chloe Cole began transitioning at the age of 13, undergoing hormone therapy and a double mastectomy by 15. By 16, Chloe regretted her decision and began the difficult journey of detransitioning. Today, she advocates for a more cautious approach to transitioning, arguing that children lack the capacity to fully understand the consequences of these irreversible decisions. Her story is a rallying cry for those who believe that transitioning should not be rushed, especially for minors.

- **B. Richie's Story: The Consequences of Hasty Decisions**

    Richie, who transitioned after only two brief consultations, now describes himself as a "neutered male." He regrets undergoing surgeries that permanently altered his body and feels alienated from both his past and present selves. Richie's story illustrates how quickly some medical professionals move forward with gender-affirming treatments, often without a comprehensive understanding of the patient's mental health needs.

- **C. The Grief of Losing Motherhood: Elizabeth's Story**

    Elizabeth underwent a double mastectomy as a teenager, believing that transitioning to male would resolve her discomfort. Four years later, after detransitioning, she became a mother and was overwhelmed by grief when she realized she could never breastfeed her newborn. The pain of losing that fundamental experience of nurturing her child haunts her, making it difficult for her to fully embrace her role as a mother.

VI. The Lack of Support and Resources for Detransitioners

Despite the growing number of individuals choosing to detransition, support resources remain scarce. Detransitioners often find that the medical and mental health communities that once supported their transition are unprepared or unwilling to help them through the reversal process.

- **A. Limited Access to Healthcare**

    Finding doctors who understand the needs of detransitioners is a significant challenge. Many detransitioners report being dismissed or misunderstood by healthcare providers, leaving them to navigate their physical health issues alone.

- **B. Inadequate Mental Health Resources**

    Mental health support specifically tailored to detransitioners is virtually non-existent. Many therapists lack the training or willingness to address the unique challenges detransitioners face, leaving them feeling abandoned and unsupported.

VII. Moving Forward: A Call for a More Cautious Approach

The stories of detransitioners highlight a critical need for a more cautious approach to gender-affirming care, particularly for minors. Before considering irreversible medical interventions, it is essential to ensure that individuals are fully informed, supported, and given the time to explore their identity without pressure.

- **A. Implementing Comprehensive Psychological Support**

Every young person experiencing gender dysphoria should receive comprehensive psychological care before any medical intervention is considered. This includes addressing underlying mental health issues and ensuring that the decision to transition is not influenced by social or external pressures.

- **B. Providing Informed Consent and a Clear Understanding of Consequences**

Informed consent must include a detailed explanation of the potential risks and consequences of transitioning, including the possibility of regret and the challenges of detransitioning.

VIII. Conclusion: Listening to the Voices of Detransitioners

Detransitioners' stories serve as a powerful reminder that transitioning is not always a solution and that, in some cases, it creates more problems than it resolves. These individuals deserve to be heard, supported, and acknowledged. By listening to their voices, we can begin to build a more compassionate and balanced approach to gender identity that prioritizes the health and happiness of every individual—regardless of where they are in their journey.

Chapter 12: Restoring Balance: Parental Rights, Responsibility, and Children's Well-Being - Reader Objectives

1. **Understand the Foundational Role of Family in Society:**
   - Recognize the family as the core building block of society, shaping individual identities and broader cultural values.
   - Explore how external forces such as social media, educational policies, and governmental interventions are challenging the traditional parent-child relationship.
2. **Learn the Importance of Strengthening Parental Rights:**
   - Understand the need for transparency and parental involvement in decisions impacting children's education and identity.
   - Examine policies and strategies that empower parents, ensuring that they remain active participants in guiding their children's upbringing and development.
3. **Explore Strategies for Maintaining Parental Involvement:**
   - Discover practical approaches to stay engaged and connected with children despite economic pressures and time constraints.
   - Learn how dedicated family time, open communication, and awareness of online activities can help maintain strong parent-child bonds.
4. **Evaluate the Role of Schools and Educational Institutions:**
   - Analyze the role of schools as centers of education rather than battlegrounds for ideological influence.
   - Discuss how restoring trust between parents and educators can help create a balanced, non-ideological learning environment that supports diverse perspectives.
5. **Understand the Economic Impact on Family Dynamics:**
   - Recognize how financial pressures and demanding work schedules contribute to a weakened family structure, leading to reduced parental oversight and involvement.
   - Examine policies such as flexible work hours, paid parental leave, and affordable childcare that can empower families and strengthen parental influence.
6. **Address the Challenges of Parenting in the Digital Age:**
   - Understand how the digital landscape—social media platforms, influencers, and online communities—can shape children's values and perceptions, often counteracting parental guidance.
   - Learn strategies to navigate the digital world, set healthy boundaries, and educate children on safe online behavior to counter negative influences.
7. **Explore Ways to Restore Parental Authority and Autonomy:**
   - Examine the broader societal shift where the state and institutions are increasingly taking over roles traditionally held by parents.
   - Consider how parents can reclaim their role as primary decision-makers, advocating for their rights in educational and healthcare decisions.
8. **Focus on the Well-Being of Children:**
   - Advocate for a balanced approach that respects children's autonomy while ensuring that parental authority and guidance remain central to their development.
   - Highlight the need for collaboration between parents, educators, and the community to create a supportive environment that prioritizes children's overall well-being.
9. **Analyze How to Rebuild the Parent-School Partnership:**

- Promote open communication and trust between parents and educators to ensure that the school environment aligns with the values and expectations of families.
- Encourage policies that provide parents with access to curricula, lesson plans, and school activities to maintain transparency and collaboration.

10. **Reinforce the Family's Role as the Cornerstone of Child Development:**
    - Emphasize the irreplaceable role of parents in nurturing, guiding, and protecting their children, ensuring that families are supported rather than undermined by external forces.
    - Call for a reaffirmation of the family's position as the primary unit of socialization, where children are equipped with the values, wisdom, and emotional security needed for healthy development.

11. **Promote a Path Forward that Restores Balance:**
    - Advocate for societal and policy changes that recognize and respect the fundamental rights of parents to guide their children's upbringing.
    - Support efforts to create educational and social systems that collaborate with families rather than working against them, ensuring that the next generation grows up in a supportive, well-balanced environment.

Chapter 12: Restoring Balance: Parental Rights, Responsibility, and Children's Well-Being

Introduction: The Foundation of Family

The relationship between parents and children forms the bedrock of society, shaping not only individual identities but also the cultural fabric of entire communities. However, this vital bond is increasingly being tested by external influences, ranging from social media and online platforms to educational policies and governmental interventions. These forces have begun to pull families apart, leading to an environment where parents often feel sidelined, and children are left without the guidance and protection that a strong family unit provides. The need to restore a healthy balance between parental rights, responsibilities, and the well-being of children has never been more urgent.

1. Strengthening Parental Rights: The Need for Transparency and Oversight

Parents have a fundamental right to be involved in their children's lives, especially when it comes to their education, social interactions, and overall development. Yet, the modern educational environment, influenced by ideologically driven agendas, often undermines this right by keeping parents out of the loop. One of the most concerning trends is the implementation of policies that encourage children to adopt new identities, experiment with gender roles, or make significant social changes—sometimes without informing their parents.

This exclusion of parents from critical decisions about their children's mental and emotional development is not only harmful but can also lead to a breakdown of trust within the family unit. Even more troubling is the rise of online influencers who actively encourage children to withhold information from their families, presenting parents as barriers to self-expression rather than essential sources of guidance and support.

To counteract this, parents must reassert their role in guiding their children's upbringing by demanding transparency within educational institutions. This includes pushing for policies that:

- **Require schools to inform parents** of any significant changes in a child's identity or social behavior.
- **Provide access to curricula, lesson plans, and resources** used in classrooms, ensuring that parents are fully aware of what is being taught.
- **Ensure parental consent** for participation in sensitive topics or activities that touch on personal identity, gender, or sexuality.

2. The Importance of Active Involvement: Being Present and Aware

The modern world has introduced unprecedented challenges for families. Rising costs of living, economic pressures, and increased demands on parents' time mean that children are often spending their formative years in the care of others, whether it be schools, aftercare programs, or even unsupervised online spaces. This physical and emotional distance can weaken familial bonds, making it easier for outside influences to shape a child's values and worldview.

It is therefore critical for parents to remain actively involved in their children's lives, even when faced with these obstacles. Strategies to maintain a strong connection include:

- **Regular communication:** Engage in meaningful conversations about your child's daily experiences, thoughts, and feelings.
- **Setting aside dedicated family time:** Prioritize activities that strengthen your relationship, such as family dinners, game nights, or shared hobbies.
- **Monitoring online interactions:** Understand what platforms your children are using, who they are interacting with, and what content they are consuming.

For those who can afford it, alternatives such as private schooling or homeschooling may provide environments where parents have more control over what their children are exposed to. While not an option for everyone, these choices underscore the need for families to be proactive in maintaining influence and guidance over their children's development.

3. The Role of Schools: Restoring the Purpose of Education

Schools should be sanctuaries of academic growth, critical thinking, and character building. Yet, in recent years, they have become battlegrounds for competing ideologies, straining the relationship between parents and educators. Many parents now view schools with suspicion, concerned that what is being taught does not align with their values or the best interests of their children.

To restore trust, schools must focus on their primary mission: educating children in a balanced, non-ideological environment that encourages diverse perspectives. This involves:

- **Establishing clear boundaries** around political and social content, ensuring that students are not pressured to adopt any particular ideology.
- **Engaging parents as partners** in the educational process, rather than sidelining them.
- **Emphasizing real-world skills** that prepare children for adulthood, rather than promoting social agendas that are disconnected from practical realities.

4. The Economic Impact: How Financial Pressures Affect Family Dynamics

The erosion of family cohesion is often driven by economic pressures. With both parents working long hours to make ends meet, many children are left in the care of schools or aftercare programs, resulting in less parental oversight and involvement. This distance can weaken the parent-child relationship, leaving children more susceptible to external influences.

Addressing this issue means not just focusing on parental rights in schools, but also tackling the broader societal and economic pressures that make it difficult for parents to be present. Policies that support families—such as flexible working hours, paid parental leave, and affordable childcare—are essential for empowering parents to play a more active role in their children's lives.

5. A Focus on Responsibility: Parenting in the Digital Age

The digital age has added a new layer of complexity to parenting. Social media platforms, YouTube personalities, and influencers have direct access to children, often promoting values and lifestyles that are at odds with what parents are trying to instill. Worse, some influencers actively encourage children to see their parents as obstacles to be overcome, rather than as sources of wisdom and love.

To protect children in this environment, parents must:

- **Educate themselves** on the digital landscape.
- **Understand the platforms** their children are using and the content they are consuming.
- **Set boundaries** around screen time and online interactions.

While it's impossible to shield children from all negative influences, being aware and engaged gives parents a better chance of counteracting harmful messages and providing a safe space for children to express their thoughts and concerns.

6. Restoring Parental Authority: The Fight for Autonomy in Child-Rearing

The erosion of parental authority is a symptom of a broader societal shift where the family is no longer seen as the primary unit of socialization. Instead, the state, educational institutions, and even online communities have taken on roles that traditionally belonged to parents. This shift disrupts the natural hierarchy of the family, leaving children adrift and more susceptible to external pressures.

To restore balance, it is essential for parents to reclaim their authority by:

- **Asserting their role** as the primary decision-makers in their children's lives.
- **Pushing back against policies** that exclude parents from critical decisions.
- **Advocating for parental rights** in education and healthcare.

7. Prioritizing Children's Well-Being: The Need for a Balanced Approach

Restoring balance is not about choosing between parental authority and children's autonomy. It's about creating an environment where children can grow, learn, and explore under the guidance of those who love them most. This balanced approach requires parents to be informed and involved, educators to be transparent and respectful, and society to recognize the family as the cornerstone of a child's well-being.

Conclusion: The Path Forward

The role of the family has been challenged in unprecedented ways, but the solution lies in reaffirming the importance of the parent-child bond. By focusing on parental rights, increasing involvement, and advocating for balanced education, we can restore the critical role of the family in shaping the next generation. Only by standing firm in our responsibilities as parents, educators, and community members can we build a future where children are free to grow into healthy, well-adjusted adults, equipped with the values and wisdom that only a strong family foundation can provide.

Chapter 13: Guiding Children in Understanding Gender Identity, Responsibility, and Societal Roles - Reader Objectives

1. **Learn How to Approach Conversations on Gender Identity and Biological Differences:**
    - Understand the need for a balanced approach when discussing gender identity and biological differences with children.
    - Explore strategies for guiding children through phases of identity exploration without overemphasizing or dismissing their experiences.
2. **Develop Methods to Foster Critical Thinking and Open Dialogue:**
    - Encourage an environment where children feel comfortable expressing their thoughts and asking questions about gender and identity.
    - Provide age-appropriate information that respects biological realities while allowing for healthy exploration and learning.
3. **Examine the Role of Schools in Gender Identity Education:**
    - Understand the impact of ideologically driven narratives in schools and how they can create confusion for children.
    - Learn about policies and practices that restore neutrality in classrooms and maintain schools as safe spaces for academic growth, critical thinking, and personal development.
4. **Explore Solutions for Strengthening Parental Oversight in Education:**
    - Learn how parents can advocate for transparency within educational institutions and gain access to curricula, lesson plans, and classroom resources.
    - Discover practical strategies for fostering a collaborative relationship between parents and schools, ensuring alignment in teaching sensitive topics.
5. **Understand the Connection Between Liberty, Responsibility, and Societal Roles:**
    - Teach children that true liberty is intrinsically linked to personal responsibility and social roles.
    - Explore ways to instill respect for various professions and the societal systems that enable freedom, helping children develop an appreciation for the infrastructure that supports a healthy society.
6. **Reintroduce Practical Skills and Civic Education for Well-Rounded Development:**
    - Assess the importance of reintroducing courses in financial literacy, home economics, and civic education to prepare children for the complexities of adult life.
    - Develop a curriculum that includes practical life skills, such as budgeting, understanding taxes, basic trades, and civic engagement.
7. **Build Stronger Family Units Through Active Parental Involvement:**
    - Examine the critical role of family in counteracting confusion and providing stability for children.
    - Implement actionable steps for parents to stay informed and involved in their child's education and online interactions, ensuring they remain the primary source of guidance and support.
8. **Promote Open Communication and Emotional Support in the Family:**
    - Create a home environment where children feel safe to express themselves without fear of judgment.

- Learn how to model positive values, such as empathy, responsibility, and critical thinking, through everyday actions and behaviors.
9. **Prepare Children for Adulthood with a Strong Foundation of Personal and Civic Responsibility:**
    - Teach children to understand their role in society and the importance of contributing positively to their communities.
    - Explore strategies for helping children build resilience, confidence, and a sense of purpose within a balanced framework of personal freedom and responsibility.
10. **Understand the Importance of Neutrality and Diverse Perspectives in Education:**
    - Advocate for schools to maintain neutrality on sensitive topics and to provide diverse viewpoints that allow children to develop their own informed opinions.
    - Promote a culture of thoughtful debate and discussion that respects differing perspectives and fosters intellectual growth.
11. **Implement Strategies for Reducing Ideological Influence in the Classroom:**
    - Learn how to set clear boundaries for teachers and educators regarding the introduction of personal ideologies into the classroom.
    - Develop policies that emphasize academic subjects, critical thinking, and character-building over social agendas.
12. **Reaffirm the Role of Parents in Shaping Children's Values and Identity:**
    - Recognize the need to restore parental authority in guiding children's personal and educational development.
    - Advocate for policies and practices that protect parental rights in healthcare and education, ensuring that the family remains the cornerstone of a child's well-being.
13. **Create a Supportive Framework for Guiding Children Through Identity and Societal Roles:**
    - Provide parents and educators with a roadmap for addressing complex topics like gender identity, personal responsibility, and societal roles.
    - Promote a balanced and informed approach that respects both the child's autonomy and the parents' role in nurturing and guiding their development.
14. **Foster a Healthy Balance of Freedom, Responsibility, and Growth for Children:**
    - Understand that guiding children is not about choosing between liberty and control, but about creating a supportive environment that fosters healthy growth and self-discovery.
    - Implement strategies for empowering children to explore, learn, and develop under the guidance of trusted adults who prioritize their long-term well-being.

Chapter 13: Guiding Children in Understanding Gender Identity, Responsibility, and Societal Roles

Introduction: Navigating Complexities in Modern Society

In today's world, conversations around gender identity, responsibility, and societal roles have become increasingly complex and often contentious. The rise of various ideological movements has created an environment where discussing gender differences, biological realities, and traditional roles can be seen as taboo. This chapter aims to provide a roadmap for parents and educators on how to guide children through these sensitive topics while also instilling a strong sense of personal responsibility, liberty, and practical skills that prepare them for adulthood.

1. A Balanced Approach: Teaching Biological Differences and Gender Identity

One of the biggest challenges facing parents and educators is how to address gender identity and biological differences without falling into the trap of either dismissiveness or over-affirmation. The goal should be to foster an understanding of the natural distinctions between boys and girls, men and women, while acknowledging that children go through phases of exploration.

Key Principles for Guiding Children Through Phases of Identity Exploration:

- **Create an Open Environment:** Allow children to express themselves and ask questions about gender and identity. It is important to provide them with age-appropriate information that aligns with biological realities and social context without overwhelming them.
- **Avoid Overemphasis on Gender Labels:** If a child expresses interest in exploring a different identity, treat it with the same weight as any other developmental phase. It should not be overly celebrated or treated as a definitive statement of their future identity.
- **Emphasize Long-Term Thinking:** Teach children to think about how decisions made today can affect their future. When children express a desire to transition or adopt a new identity, remind them that their bodies are still developing, and it's okay to wait before making irreversible changes.

2. The Role of Schools: Keeping Political Ideology Out of Education

Schools should be centers of learning and critical thinking, not venues for promoting specific ideologies. However, in recent years, political and ideological narratives have crept into classrooms, particularly around sensitive topics like gender identity. This shift has created confusion for children and has undermined parents' confidence in the educational system.

Solutions for Restoring Neutrality in Education:

- **Implement Clear Boundaries for Teachers:** Establish policies that prevent teachers from introducing their personal ideologies into the classroom, particularly when it comes to sensitive topics like gender identity. The focus should be on teaching academic subjects and promoting critical thinking.
- **Increase Parental Oversight:** Parents should be informed about what is being taught in the classroom and have access to curriculum materials. Schools should foster a collaborative relationship with parents, rather than treating them as adversaries.
- **Encourage a Culture of Debate:** Schools should teach children to engage in thoughtful debates, exposing them to diverse viewpoints so they can form their own opinions without being swayed by a single narrative.

3. Liberty, Responsibility, and Understanding Societal Roles

The concept of liberty is often misunderstood by children, who may see it as the freedom to do whatever they want without considering the consequences. Teaching children that liberty is intrinsically linked to responsibility is essential for helping them grow into conscientious adults.

Key Values to Impart:

- **Understanding the Role of Work in Society:** Children need to appreciate that every job, whether glamorous or mundane, is essential for society's functioning. This understanding fosters respect for others and encourages a sense of duty.
- **Appreciating the Systems That Enable Freedom:** Teach children about the infrastructure, government, and societal rules that allow them to experience freedom. This helps them understand that liberty must be maintained and defended.
- **Linking Liberty to Personal Responsibility:** True freedom comes from being self-sufficient and responsible. Teach children practical skills, civic duties, and the importance of contributing positively to their communities.

4. Reintroducing Practical Skills and Civic Education

The educational system has moved away from teaching practical life skills, leaving many young people unprepared for the realities of adulthood. By reintroducing courses like financial literacy, home economics, and civic education, schools can help equip students with the tools they need to navigate the complexities of modern life.

Core Areas for Practical Education:

- **Financial Literacy:** Teach children how taxes work, how to budget, and how to save and invest money. This knowledge is crucial for building financial independence.
- **Basic Trades and Home Skills:** Offer classes in shop, cooking, sewing, and basic home repairs. This empowers children to be self-sufficient and reduces dependency on external services.
- **Understanding Politics and Civic Responsibility:** As children approach adolescence, they should be introduced to political systems, the roles of different parties, and the importance of civic engagement. A well-informed citizenry is essential for a functioning democracy.

5. Restoring Parental Involvement and Building Strong Families

The most powerful antidote to the confusion many children feel today is a strong, supportive family. Parents must be actively involved in their children's education and upbringing, ensuring that they are the primary source of guidance and support.

Actionable Steps for Parents:

- **Stay Informed and Involved:** Know what is happening in your child's school and who they are interacting with online. Regularly communicate with teachers and stay engaged in your child's learning.
- **Promote Open Communication:** Make sure your children feel comfortable coming to you with their thoughts and questions. Avoid creating an environment of judgment or dismissal.
- **Model the Values You Wish to Instill:** Children learn more from what they see than from what they are told. Model responsibility, empathy, and critical thinking in your own behavior.

Conclusion: A Path Toward Balance and Stability

Guiding children through the complexities of gender identity, personal responsibility, and societal roles requires a thoughtful and balanced approach. By focusing on education, open dialogue, and the restoration of parental authority, parents and educators can create a supportive environment where children can explore, learn, and grow under the guidance of those who care for them most.

Ultimately, this chapter calls for a return to common sense, where children are encouraged to develop critical thinking skills, respect for others, and a strong sense of self within a framework that honors both personal freedom and social responsibility. Only by working together—families, schools, and communities—can we create a future where children are prepared to face the world with confidence, resilience, and a deep appreciation for the liberties and responsibilities that define a healthy society.

Chapter 14: Addressing the Issue of Medical Protocols and Protecting Children from Ideological Manipulation - Reader Objectives

1. **Understand the Need for Reform in Medical Protocols for Children:**
    - Grasp the necessity of establishing common-sense medical guidelines that prioritize the health and safety of minors over ideological agendas.
    - Recognize the dangers of using powerful drugs like hormone blockers and cross-sex hormones on children without comprehensive long-term research.
2. **Learn About Ethical Considerations in Pediatric Medical Interventions:**
    - Explore the ethical implications of administering irreversible medical treatments to children and adolescents.
    - Understand the principle of "first, do no harm" and how current practices around gender-affirming care for minors may contradict this standard.
3. **Examine the Influence of Ideology on Medical Decisions:**
    - Identify how ideologically driven narratives can overshadow sound medical judgment in the context of gender dysphoria treatments for minors.
    - Understand how ideological pressures can lead to a rush toward transitioning without adequately exploring other therapeutic options.
4. **Evaluate the Dangers of Ideological and Social Engineering:**
    - Learn how social pressures and the glamorization of gender nonconformity can steer children toward early transitioning.
    - Explore how children may be influenced by external validation, making it difficult for them to reconsider their decisions or express doubts.
5. **Review Practical Recommendations for Medical Policy Reform:**
    - Assess key recommendations, including prohibiting the use of puberty blockers and cross-sex hormones in minors, and implementing mandatory psychological evaluations before any medical intervention.
    - Understand the need for informed consent and waiting periods even for adults considering gender-affirming treatments.
6. **Discover Strategies to Protect Children from Ideological Manipulation:**
    - Learn about policies and safeguards that can be put in place to protect children from being manipulated or rushed into irreversible decisions.
    - Understand the importance of banning ideologically driven content from schools and enforcing rigorous standards for counselors and therapists.
7. **Explore the Role of Parents in Safeguarding Their Children's Health and Well-Being:**
    - Reaffirm the critical role of parents in making informed decisions regarding their child's health and development.
    - Advocate for parental consent and transparency in medical and educational settings, ensuring that parents remain the primary guardians of their children's well-being.
8. **Analyze the Broader Societal Impact of Ideological Influence on Medical Practices:**
    - Understand how "woke" ideology has infiltrated medical institutions, leading to a shift in protocols and priorities that may not align with the best interests of children.
    - Examine the long-term societal consequences of allowing ideology to dictate medical decisions for vulnerable populations.

9. **Identify the Signs of Ideological Manipulation in Schools and Counseling:**
    - Learn how to recognize when schools or therapists may be pushing a particular narrative that conflicts with evidence-based practices.
    - Equip parents and educators with the tools to challenge and correct such behaviors, ensuring that children receive balanced and thoughtful guidance.
10. **Promote Open Dialogue and Resist Ideological Intimidation:**
    - Develop strategies for fostering open dialogue and countering the stigma surrounding those who question prevailing narratives around gender identity and medical interventions.
    - Advocate for the protection of free speech and respectful discourse, encouraging communities to discuss these sensitive topics without fear of ostracism or reprisal.
11. **Support a Balanced and Thoughtful Approach to Identity Exploration:**
    - Advocate for policies and practices that give children space to explore their identities without feeling pressured to make drastic decisions.
    - Promote therapeutic exploration and support for children experiencing gender dysphoria, rather than fast-tracking them toward medical interventions.
12. **Implement Long-Term Oversight and Accountability in Medical Institutions:**
    - Push for increased oversight and accountability in medical institutions, ensuring that standards of care prioritize the well-being of the child over ideological conformity.
    - Advocate for independent reviews of medical protocols and guidelines to prevent the undue influence of ideologically driven narratives.
13. **Encourage Legal and Policy Reforms to Protect Minors:**
    - Support legal initiatives that prohibit irreversible medical interventions for minors until they reach adulthood.
    - Advocate for policies that ensure minors are given comprehensive psychological support and a thorough understanding of the potential risks and outcomes before considering any medical path.
14. **Commit to a Child-Centric Approach in Healthcare and Education:**
    - Reaffirm the importance of prioritizing children's health and long-term well-being over short-term social validation or ideological goals.
    - Encourage healthcare and educational systems to adopt a more child-centric approach, focusing on developmentally appropriate and ethically sound practices.
15. **Establish a Framework for Supporting Families in Navigating Gender Issues:**
    - Provide resources and guidance for parents to navigate complex gender issues in a way that respects the child's development while avoiding irreversible decisions.
    - Advocate for comprehensive family counseling and support networks that empower parents and children to work through these challenges together.
16. **Resist Social and Media Pressures That Promote Early Medical Interventions:**
    - Develop a critical understanding of how media and social pressures can glamorize early transitions, pushing children toward drastic measures without considering long-term impacts.
    - Learn strategies for resisting these pressures and promoting a more measured and cautious approach to gender identity exploration.
17. **Foster a Culture of Patient-Centric Care in the Medical Community:**
    - Advocate for a shift away from ideology-driven practices and toward patient-centric care that respects the complexity of each child's unique developmental journey.
    - Promote policies that prioritize comprehensive mental health support and evidence-based approaches in dealing with gender dysphoria.

Chapter 14: Addressing the Issue of Medical Protocols and Protecting Children from Ideological Manipulation

Introduction: Prioritizing Children's Health and Well-Being

When it comes to medical treatments for children, protocols must be guided by the fundamental principle of protecting their health and development. However, in the current climate surrounding gender-affirming care, this principle is often overshadowed by ideological narratives that push children toward irreversible decisions with insufficient regard for long-term consequences. This approach not only conflicts with basic medical ethics but, in many cases, risks causing more harm than good.

The inconsistency in medical standards is startling: while over-the-counter medications are heavily regulated for children under certain ages, powerful drugs like hormone blockers and cross-sex hormones are prescribed under the guise of gender identity affirmation. These medications, designed to fundamentally alter a child's physical and mental development, are being administered despite a lack of comprehensive long-term studies on their effects. This contradiction points to a disturbing trend where ideology supersedes sound medical judgment, making a case for immediate reform in medical protocols concerning children.

1. Establishing Common-Sense Medical Guidelines

Medical protocols for children should prioritize the principle of **"first, do no harm."** The use of drugs that can have a profound and permanent impact on a child's growth and development should be strictly limited to cases with overwhelming evidence of their necessity. The idea that a child, who cannot legally consent to less significant medical treatments, could be placed on a path of permanent physiological change is not only reckless but deeply unethical.

Key Recommendations for Medical Policy Reform:

- **Prohibit the Use of Puberty Blockers and Cross-Sex Hormones in Minors:**
  Children and adolescents are still in critical stages of physical and mental development. The use of puberty blockers, cross-sex hormones, or any drug that interferes with natural growth should be strictly prohibited until the individual reaches adulthood. These treatments are being administered without sufficient long-term research on their effects, and the risks should not be borne by children who are incapable of fully informed consent.
- **Mandatory Psychological Evaluation and Counseling:**
  Children experiencing gender dysphoria should receive comprehensive psychological support and counseling before any medical intervention is considered. This evaluation should explore all potential factors contributing to their distress and ensure that other

mental health conditions are addressed first. Understanding the root causes of gender dysphoria is essential before resorting to irreversible treatments.
- **Implement Informed Consent and Waiting Periods for Adults:**
Even for adults, the decision to undergo gender-affirming treatments should come with thorough informed consent and mandatory waiting periods. This ensures that individuals have the time and space to consider the long-term implications of their choices and are not making decisions under duress or in the midst of emotional distress.

2. Recognizing Ideological Influence in Medical Decisions

At the core of the issue is the role of ideology in shaping medical protocols. What we are witnessing is a complex intersection of cultural narratives and medical practice, resulting in a system that focuses more on affirming an ideology than on safeguarding the health of patients. This is particularly evident in the aggressive push to transition children at increasingly younger ages, often without parental consent or proper oversight.

The rise of "woke" ideology in this context is troubling because it seeks to validate its beliefs through the bodies of vulnerable children. By framing gender transition as the only acceptable solution to gender dysphoria, proponents of this ideology effectively shut down any alternative approaches, such as watchful waiting or therapeutic exploration. Children expressing discomfort with their gender are often fast-tracked into medical transitions, with little consideration for potential long-term consequences.

3. The Dangers of Social and Ideological Engineering

When children are encouraged to view transitioning as the primary or even the only way to address their feelings, they are not being given the space to fully explore their identities. Instead, they are being steered toward a predetermined outcome, often under the influence of external factors.

Key Issues:

- **Normalization of Early Transitioning:**
The normalization of early transitioning and the glamorization of gender nonconformity through media and celebrity endorsements can create a feedback loop where children are drawn to these identities not out of genuine need, but because they are presented as trendy, desirable, or even heroic.
- **Emotional and Social Impact:**
The moment a child is celebrated for transitioning, they are placed on a pedestal, making it emotionally and socially difficult for them to revert to their original identity if they later have second thoughts. This creates a trap where the child's identity is manipulated and shaped by external validation rather than self-discovery.

4. The Intersection of Ideology and Infrastructure

The broader issue here is not just the medicalization of children but how "woke" ideology has infiltrated all aspects of society, from media to schools to social policy. This ideology thrives on a culture of victimhood and conflict, drawing its energy from a constant state of grievance. As a result, it is inherently destabilizing and cannot sustain the very structures it seeks to control.

5. Protecting Children from Ideological Manipulation

One of the most concerning aspects of the current trend is the targeting of children as the primary demographic for spreading these ideas. Children are impressionable and eager to conform to what they perceive as socially acceptable or desirable. Encouraging them to undergo drastic and permanent changes to their bodies in pursuit of an ideological goal is a form of manipulation that must be condemned.

Policies to Protect Children:

- **Banning Ideologically Driven Content from Schools:**
  Schools should not be venues for political indoctrination. Curricula should focus on academic learning and critical thinking rather than promoting any particular social ideology.
- **Implementing Strict Guidelines for Counseling and Therapy:**
  Therapists and counselors should be held to rigorous standards to ensure that they are not pushing a particular narrative. This includes regular oversight and a focus on evidence-based practices rather than affirming ideologies.
- **Reinforcing the Role of Parents in Educational and Medical Decisions:**
  Parents are the primary guardians of their children's well-being. Any policy that seeks to exclude them from decisions about their child's education or health should be repealed. Schools and medical institutions must be legally required to obtain parental consent and maintain transparency.

6. Standing Firm Against Ideological Intimidation

Finally, the stigma surrounding speaking out against these practices must be addressed. The tactics of shaming, ostracizing, and canceling those who dare to challenge the prevailing narrative are designed to silence dissent and maintain control. However, silence only enables the spread of harmful ideologies.

Action Steps:

- **Encouraging Open Dialogue:**
  Communities must come together to demand change and ensure that the safety and well-being of children take precedence over ideology. There should be widespread legal challenges and organized efforts to push back against policies that seek to experiment on children for ideological reasons.

Conclusion: Ensuring a Safe Future for Our Children

The primary responsibility of adults is to protect children from harm and to ensure that they grow up in an environment where they can thrive. The current trend of pushing children into irreversible medical interventions in the name of ideology is a grave violation of this responsibility. We must advocate for policies that safeguard children's health, promote a balanced approach to understanding identity, and respect the rights of parents to guide their children's upbringing.

By standing together and advocating for these changes, we can put an end to practices that risk irreparably harming young lives and restore a system that truly prioritizes the well-being and future of every child.

Glossary

Woke: A term originally used to signify awareness of social injustices and inequality, now often referring to a broader ideological framework centered on social activism.

Ideological: Relating to or concerned with ideas, beliefs, or doctrines, often in the context of political or cultural systems.

Social Justice: The pursuit of fairness and equality within society, particularly in addressing issues related to race, gender, and class disparities.

Activism: The practice of taking direct action to advocate for or against social, political, or environmental causes.

Identity: The understanding of oneself, often in relation to race, gender, ethnicity, and culture, which influences personal and collective perspectives.

Parenting: The process of raising and educating children, shaped by personal values, cultural norms, and societal expectations.

Progressive: Advocating for change, reform, or improvement, often associated with left-leaning political ideologies that emphasize equality and social justice.

Generation: A group of people born and living around the same time, sharing similar cultural and societal influences.

Beliefs: Convictions or acceptance that certain things are true or real, often shaping personal or collective values.

Critical Thinking: The objective analysis and evaluation of an issue or situation in order to form a judgment, encouraging independent thought.

Overreach: Exceeding reasonable limits, often in the context of extending control or influence beyond what is justified.

Advocacy: The act of publicly supporting or recommending a particular cause or policy.

Empathy: The ability to understand and share the feelings of others, an important component in both personal relationships and societal dynamics.

Values: Principles or standards of behavior that guide the decisions and actions of individuals and groups.

Influence: The capacity to have an effect on the character, development, or behavior of someone or something.

Boundaries: Limits that define acceptable behavior or the scope of control, important in both personal and social contexts.

Ideology: A system of ideas and ideals, especially one that forms the basis of economic or political theory and policy.

Misunderstanding: A failure to understand something correctly, often leading to conflict or confusion.

Narratives: The structured accounts or stories that convey specific meanings, shaping people's understanding of events or ideas.

Progressivism: A political or social philosophy advocating for reform and improvement, particularly in social, economic, or environmental issues.